KEW VILLAGE MARKET
COOKBOOK

100 RECIPES
celebrating our stallholders' produce

Compiled by Sarah Edington
with a foreword by David Blomfield

For the Kew Village Market stallholders, volunteers and customers, who make the first Sunday of the month so special

About the writer

Sarah Edington has lived in Kew for many years and, as a professional cook, has fed members of the royal family as well as several prime ministers and archbishops of Canterbury. She has written six books for the National Trust and won the Museum Book of the Year 2005 with *The Captain's Table, Life and Fine Dining on the Great Ocean Liners*. Her most recent, *The Complete Traditional Recipe Book,* is a definitive collection of the best in British cooking.

© 2014 Kew Village Market Community Interest Corporation
Published by the Kew Village Market CIC

Design and production by Andrew Becker Design Ltd
Printed by Samson Print

ISBN 978-0-9930250-0-6

www.kewvillagemarket.org

Contents

Foreword	7
Introduction	9
Boring but useful	10
Conversion tables	10
Beer & wine matchings	11
About Kew Village Market	106
Index of recipes	109
Supporting local charities	111
Thank yous	111

Stallholders

Avlaki Olive Oil	12
Bang Curry	16
Beech Hill Farm	18
Belle's Bonbons	22
Caffè Torelli	24
Carolyn Dawson	28
Crazy Cat's Pantry	34
La Crêpe Des Delices	38
Fidelma's Kitchen	42
Flax Farm	44
Food On The Hill	48
Love By Cake	50
Lusobrazil	54
Madame Macaroon	56
Noggin Farm	60
Norbiton Cheese Co	66
Nut Knowle Farm	70
The Nutty Lady	74
Oliver's Wholefood Store	76
The Portland Scallop Company	80
Ruben's Bakehouse	84
C&S Stileman	88
Strawberry Dream	92
Sugarmaddy Cakes	94
Thee Olive Tree	98
Winterbourne Game	102

Foreword

Local historian David Blomfield looks at Kew's market gardeners, whose flourishing businesses once supplied all London with fruit and vegetables.

Kew Village Market may have seen the Diamond Jubilee of Elizabeth II but its two forebears, Kew's market gardens and the agricultural village of Kew Green, date mostly from the age of the first Elizabeth.

Today's market lies on the borderline between these two distinct areas, which make up the village as we now know it, and inherits much from both of them. For some four centuries, one half of Kew – the triangle now marked by the river, the A316, and a line down the Sandycombe Road leading straight on to the riverbank – was farmed commercially as market gardens. Meanwhile the other half of Kew, except for the private estate that is now Kew Gardens, supported a traditional self-sufficient village community, centred on the Green.

The market gardens were devoted to the production of vegetables and fruit. The most valuable crop was asparagus, its profit per acre being ten times that of wheat. Other vegetables and flowers were also in demand, as explained by Maisie Brown in her *Market Gardens of Barnes and Mortlake*. (This area of Kew then lay within Mortlake.) 'The ridges and alleys between the asparagus were planted with french beans in early summer and coleworts [cabbages] in the autumn. Any spare space was filled with radishes and lettuce, while odd corners were filled with mint, sage and parsley, as well as narcissi, daffodils, bluebells and lily-of-the-valley.'

This market garden business – and it was big business – was run by a small number of master gardeners, who catered for the huge appetites for what then were delicacies, and required equally huge quantities of manure for the intensive cultivation of successive crops. The inhabitants of London supplied both the manure and the appetites. Every night dung barges, piled high with the city's 'night soil' along with road sweepings and horse manure, would work their way up river to a wharf at the end of the lane from West Hall. At the same time a line of carts, piled equally high with vegetables, and led by women and children, would trail through the night to Covent Garden.

The master gardeners' names are still well known in Kew: they are displayed on the streets signs that mark the fields where they worked. William Atwood was the secretary of the Market Gardeners Association, and he and his family lived in Leyborne Lodge for some 150 years. George Bessant, his daughters and grandson worked from Brick Farm Stables in West Hall Road for over 100 years, and Mr and Mrs Dancer were famous for the quality of their asparagus.

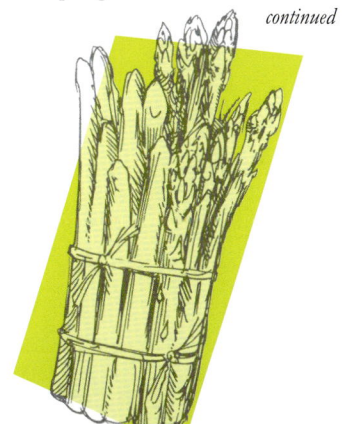

continued

continued

So long as the market gardens flourished, so did the more varied parallel economy of the village community around Kew Green. Here the villagers pollarded the willows to make hurdles that would create 'weirs' in the river from which they would suspend their fishing nets. (Hence the name of Westerley Ware, where they would hang their nets up to dry.) The fishing for many years was exceptional, but it did not last. By 1850 pollution had killed all but the eels.

Agriculture outlasted the fisheries, with nursery gardens patronised by the rich around the Green, and fields of wheat along Kew Road. Meanwhile the Green was used in traditional fashion for grazing cattle. It was fenced, and householders with property of rentable value of £12 could graze one animal; those with £50 could graze three. This right was valuable, for up to 1900 there were at least two butchers eager to share the profits, one in Mortlake Terrace and another opposite at no 9 the Green. Both had slaughterhouses behind their shops.

By then the market garden business had collapsed. From the 1850s the trains began to bring in fresh vegetables to London from less expensive fields. The Thameside gardeners could not compete. For a few decades they survived by concentrating on fruit, with orchards that produced an upper crop of apples, pears and plums, grown on dwarf stocks, along with a lower crop of gooseberries, black and red currants. Here too, eventually, the market gardeners fell prey to the brutal force of the market. Houses were wanted near London.

The landlords – in Kew's case almost all the land was owned by the Leyborne Pophams, absentee landlords living in Wiltshire – found that they could make bigger profits through selling their land for housing. The market gardeners moved west.

What then is the legacy left by our forebears? The allotments of Short Lots (and the annual Horticultural Show) have kept the spirit and the expertise of the market gardeners alive. Asparagus and fruit trees, and the occasional walnut tree, still survive stubbornly in our gardens.

There may too be a legacy from even further back, and from an exceptionally famous resident. In his *Herbal* of 1511, William Turner wrote of the chickpea, 'I have it my garden at Kew'. Have you? Turner is known as the Father of English Botany. We do not know where he lived in Kew. You may have the answer.

Introduction

Every first Sunday of the month, between ten in the morning and two in the afternoon, cars are banned from Kew Village and in their place comes a host of colourful stalls. Some sell hand-made local crafts, but mostly they sell food. And what delicious food — meat, fish, vegetables, cheeses, pork pies, pâtés, tarts, cakes and confectionery, olives and artisan breads.

You can shop here to cook, safe in the knowledge that everything is sustainably grown or reared. You can shop here to avoid cooking. Pies, soups, salads are all hand-made. French galettes, pancakes and the best sort of bangers and burgers are cooked right in front of you. Sunday lunch has never been easier.

All the recipes in this book can be cooked using ingredients obtainable at the market. Some are very simple, some less so — but they are all rewarding. Many of the recipes come from the Kew Village Market stallholders, people who love what they do and care what they sell, and others are my favourites, made even more special when cooked with ingredients of such quality.

We hope this book will inspire you — to come to the market, to buy, to cook, to eat, to drink and to enjoy.

Sarah Edington

Boring but useful

Although many of the recipes give the approximate number of people the quantity will feed, please remember, appetites vary.

I have given cooking times and temperatures but find from personal experience that these vary in different stoves so do regard them as an indication rather than an order. Test meat to see that it is tender by trying a piece. The best way to test if a cake is cooked is to plunge a stainless-steel skewer into the middle. If it comes out clean, the cake is cooked. Cakes and biscuits must be cooled completely either on a wire tray or in their cooking tin and only stored when they are cold.

In all the recipes, unless otherwise stated, all spoonfuls are level, standard spoon measurements: a tablespoon (tbs) = 15g or 15ml; and a teaspoon (tsp) = 5g or 5ml. All eggs are medium sized and the percentages given in the beer notes refer to ABV (alcohol by volume).

Always sift the flour you are using, even if it doesn't say so. There are recipes which will not work unless you do, and it is always better to be on the safe side.

Please be sure to read the recipe right through before you start, not least to find out what would best accompany the finished dish.

Finally, the stallholders are all experts in how to cook what they sell and, as you would expect with personal recipes, their methods vary. In this book we've respected their differences rather than making the recipes consistent at the expense of individuality and authenticity.

Metric to imperial conversions

Don't switch between metric and imperial within one recipe. There will be small discrepancies between equivalent weights and you could end up with the wrong proportions of ingredients.

Weight		Volume		
10g	¼ oz	1.25ml	¼ tsp	
15g	½ oz	2.5ml	½ tsp	
25g	1 oz	5ml	1 tsp	
50g	1¾ oz	15ml	1 tbs	
75g	2¾ oz	30ml	1 fl oz	
100g	3½ oz	50ml	2 fl oz	
150g	5½ oz	100ml	3⅓ fl oz	
175g	6 oz	150ml	5 fl oz	¼ pint
200g	7 oz	200ml	7 fl oz	⅓ pint
225g	8 oz	300ml	10 fl oz	½ pint
250g	9 oz	500ml	18 fl oz	
275g	9¾ oz	600ml	20 fl oz	1 pint
300g	10½ oz	700ml		1¼ pints
350g	12 oz	850ml		1½ pints
375g	13 oz	1 litre		1¾ pints
400g	14 oz	1.2 litres		2 pints
425g	15 oz			
450g	1lb			
500g	1lb 2oz			
700g	1lb 8oz			
750g	1lb 10oz			
1kg	2lb 4oz			
1.25kg	2lb 12oz			
1.5kg	3lb 5oz			
2kg	4lb 8oz			
2.25kg	5lb			
2.5kg	5lb 8oz			
3kg	6lb 8oz			

Beer & wine matchings

Craft-brewed beers and fine wines complement good food, so we are very lucky that regular stallholder Real Ale Ltd and The Good Wine Shop in Royal Parade have used their time and expertise to suggest the perfect beer and/or wine to accompany many of the recipes.

Real Ale Ltd

Real Ale Ltd started with a beer shop in 2005, with the aim of introducing to a wider audience the high quality, but often unknown, craft beer and ciders being produced by British micro-breweries. They now source from across the world, and also apply their ethos of showcasing small producers to a wide range of wines and spirits.

Real Ale really know their stuff – deservedly they were deemed Best Retail Business in the Community at the 2013 Richmond Business Awards. They stock a beer for every occasion and every taste – they have beers which are light or dark, rich or delicate, still or aerated. Do visit their stall at the market or the shop in Twickenham (see www.realale.com for details). At either place there will be someone knowledgeable to discuss your particular requirements. You can even join other beer enthusiasts at monthly tutored tastings, where you can meet the brewer. It has never been a better time to be a beer drinker!

The Good Wine Shop

When Mark Wrigglesworth took over The Good Wine Shop in December 2004, he wanted to provide an alternative to all the branded wines that had flooded the market. So he started to source interesting and quirky wines from small producers where wines have a back-story and a sense of place. He pledged that he wouldn't sell a bottle of wine unless he had personally tasted it and enjoyed it.

Today Mark stocks around 850 different bottles of wine, craft beers and artisan spirits (you can get a flavour of his range at www.thegoodwineshop.co.uk) but his ethos remains the same: everything sold at The Good Wine Shop can be vouched for by Mark himself or one of his knowledgeable staff.

from Avlaki Olive Oil

Lovingly grown in the Greek sun, picked and milled with with care and bottled, unfiltered, just four weeks from picking – no wonder Avlaki Organic Extra Virgin Olive Oils tastes so good!

Avlaki is a tiny artisanal operation, a partnership between the painter Deborah MacMillan and the writer and broadcaster Natalie Wheen. They have two subtly different oils to choose from, both grown on the island of Lesvos in south-facing fields: Agatheri Groves are 600 metres above the sea, giving a subtle oil with delicate flavours; whereas Avlaki Groves are in a sunny, sheltered position just above sea level, which makes for a robustly flavourful oil. (Visit the website www.oliveoilavlaki to find out more.)

Here Natalie shares some of the ways that Avlaki Extra Virgin Olive Oils can make simple dishes special, and recipes for three delicious dips follow.

Marinade for beef

Mix 2 tbs extra virgin olive oil, some freshly ground pepper, 1 tbs finely chopped onion, 1 tbs chopped parsley and/or oregano. Turn the meat in the oil mix and let it stand for at least one hour, preferably longer. Grill or fry the meat, using the marinade to baste it.

Marinade for lamb

Mix 2 tbs extra virgin olive oil with dried chopped chilli (it's your choice how hot you want it), 2 finely chopped cloves of garlic and the zest of half a lemon. Rub this mix into the meat and leave it for at least two hours and preferably longer (overnight perhaps). Roast or barbecue the meat.

Piquant dressing for sliced cold meat

Mix 2 tbs extra virgin olive oil with the grated rind and juice of half a lemon, 2 tsp capers, 1 tsp chopped gherkin, 1 chopped garlic clove and salt and pepper to taste. Spread or pour it over the meat slices. Cover the dish, keep it in a cool place for several hours to infuse the slices of meat and serve at room temperature.

Olive mashed potato

Use extra virgin olive oil instead of butter and milk to make a really tasty mash. Drizzle it in as you break up the potato. Check for pepper and salt. Why not add chopped parsley or chives or grated Parmesan cheese? Mash as you have never tasted it before!

With steamed vegetables, pasta or soups

A drizzle of extra virgin olive oil just before serving enhances the flavour of steamed vegetables, enriches a pasta dish and lifts a soup into something very special.

Olive oil & vinegar dressing

Extra virgin oil gives the best flavour when mixed at a proportion of 3-to-1: 3 tbs oil to 1 tbs wine or cider vinegar/balsamic vinegar/lemon juice. Add pepper and salt to taste and you have the simplest of dressings. Make more than you need, put it in a screw-top jar and it will keep for several days. Use it plain or add any of the following: Dijon mustard and/or a small amount of sugar, chopped garlic, chopped herbs such as flat-leafed parsley, basil (remember to tear the leaves of basil, not chop them with a knife – that way they won't blacken and wilt), dill leaves, chives, oregano or chervil to taste. Alternatively the basic dressing, made with balsamic vinegar, is perfect just as it is for tomato salad.

For baking fish

Take a piece of baking foil large enough to make a parcel of a single whole fish (such as brill or dover sole) or a single portion of fish fillet or steak (salmon, turbot, cod or haddock are good). Brush the foil with olive oil, place the fish on the foil and drizzle more oil on the top. Cut a lemon into quarters and then again. Squeeze the lemon from one slice on to the fish. (Serve the second lemon slice with the fish.) Add chopped dill, fennel and/or parsley. Pepper and salt the fish and close up the parcel. Roast in a hot oven *(200C/fan 180/gas 6)* for 20 minutes only for the whole fish and 10 minutes for the single portions. Turn the oven off after 20/10 minutes but leave the fish in the oven for at least another 10 minutes. Open the parcels, place the fish on the plate and pour the contents of the parcel over it. Serve with a lemon slice to squeeze over, steamed or boiled new potatoes and a green leaf salad.

Hummus

Did you know that the British eat more hummus than any other country? Neither did I. Here is a recipe that is simplicity itself. It can be as chunky or as smooth as you like. The one fact not to forget is to use a really special extra virgin olive oil – the better the oil, the tastier the hummus. Serve it with pitta breads, crusty French bread or chopped vegetables.

Serves 6

2 tins (400g each) of chick peas

Grated rind and juice of a large lemon

2 tbs tahini (sesame paste)

4 cloves of garlic, crushed

2 tbs extra virgin olive oil

Pepper and salt to taste

Paprika and flat leaf parsley to garnish

Drain 1 tin of chick peas and put into a blender or food processor, along with the second tin with its liquid, the lemon juice and rind, the tahini, the garlic cloves and 1 tbs of the olive oil.

Pulse the mixture to make a rough hummus or blend until smooth. Season with pepper and salt and either pile the mix into bowl to be used as dip or serve it the Middle Eastern way, spread out on a plate. Either way, fork up the surface and drizzle the rest of the oil over the top.

Dust with paprika and sprinkle with a little chopped parsley to serve.

NB You can't freeze this hummus, but it will keep for up to 5 days in the fridge.

Broad bean dip

Serve with toasted pitta bread or crisp French bread.

Serves 4
as a starter or side dish

400g broad beans, fresh or frozen
4 tbs extra virgin olive oil
Grated rind and juice of ½ a lemon
2 stems of fresh mint, torn into shreds

Either steam or simmer the broad beans for about 8 minutes. Drain and let them cool a little, then pop the beans out of their grey-green skins. Put them in a blender or food processor and pulse them until they break up.

Then put the blender/food processor on automatic and pour in 3 tbs of oil and the lemon juice and rind while the machine is running. You should have a smoothish purée.

Check for pepper and salt, then stir in the mint and the last tablespoonful of oil just before serving.

Aubergine salad or Baba Ganoush

We probably think of a salad as being made of leaves of raw vegetables. Baba Ganoush is quite different. The aubergine is roasted until the flesh is soft and then combined with garlic, oil and lemon. The resulting purée is spread thickly over a plate with more oil drizzled over the top. Absolutely delicious! Serve it with bread, pittas and/or dipping vegetables, such as batons of carrot, chunks of cucumber, celery sticks and button mushrooms, to scoop up the salad.

Serves 4
as a starter or side dish

1 large aubergine
Grated rind and juice of ½ a lemon
4 tbs extra virgin olive oil
2 cloves of garlic, crushed
Pepper and salt
Flat-leaf parsley to garnish

Preheat the oven to 200C/ fan 180/gas 6.

Roast the aubergine until the skin is black (this can take 20 minutes or more). When you can feel that the flesh is soft, take it out of the oven and let it cool a little, then strip the skin off. You will be left with a pulp, which at this point is stringy.

Put the pulp into a food processor or blender and pulse it with 3 tbs of oil, the lemon rind and juice and the crushed garlic cloves. Check for pepper and salt, then tip the purée on to a flat plate. Spread it out and mark the top with a fork.

Drizzle the last tablespoonful of oil over the top and, just before you are going to serve it, scatter a few parsley leaves over the top.

from Bang Curry

'My family moved to Britain in the 1960s and they brought with them a real passion and skill for Bangladeshi cooking,' says Shelly Nuruzzaman. 'I was transfixed by the sight and scents of the spices in my mother's kitchen, and over time I developed a deep understanding of Bangladeshi cuisine. I learned to copy and improvise on spice blends and use cooking methods adopted from my home country, Britain.

'From that understanding, the idea for Bang Curry was born. The Bang Spice Mixes are based on traditional recipes used by generations of my Bangladeshi family. The spicing in these recipes has been tested, refined and transformed into the 3-Step Spice Mixes which I sell on the stall.'

Shelly's idea is a winner. Buy the mix, follow her three steps and you will cook an authentically delicious Bangladeshi curry. If this tempts you to know more, visit her website (www.bangcurry.com) and sign up for one of her cookery lessons to receive expert instruction from Shelly.

Fish korma with tomatoes

Shelly's subtle spicing suits any firm fish. Keep your nerve and cook the fish for just the three minutes! The texture will be perfect.

Serves 4
4 tbs vegetable oil
30g fresh ginger, peeled and chopped fine
3 cloves of garlic, peeled and chopped fine
200g onions, peeled and chopped
1 Korma Spice Mix
500g fresh tomatoes, sliced
500g fresh firm fish (such as cod, salmon, John Dory or monkfish)
200ml coconut milk
Salt to taste
A handful of fresh coriander

For all the curries
THE GOOD WINE SHOP RECOMMENDS
Fratelli-Akluj Chenin Blanc from Maharastra in India. (If you want a wine match for curry, why not go straight to the horse's mouth?) This delicious white Chenin has just the right balance of fresh acidity and residual sweetness to cope with spicy foods.

Heat the oil in either a wok or a large shallow pan and fry the ginger, garlic and onions. When they are beginning to soften, add the curry mix, stir so the vegetables are all coated with it and cook for about 4 minutes.

The delicious smell will tell you when to move on to the next stage. Add the tomatoes and 100ml water. Cover the pan and simmer the curry for about 10 minutes. While it is cooking chop the fish into chunks. Stir in the coconut milk and mix it gently with the vegetables. (You can cook the curry ahead to this point and reheat it when needed.)

Bring the pan back to a simmer, then add the fish chunks very gently. Bring back to a simmer again, cover the pan and cook the curry for just 3 minutes. The fish cooks very quickly and you don't want the chunks to break up. Check for salt, chop the coriander over the curry and serve with boiled rice.

Spicy hot dry vegetable curry

Feel the heat – this is for curry lovers who want it really spicy. Vary the vegetables as you wish; you want to end up with a mixture of textures and colours.

Serves 4

- 3 tbs vegetable oil
- 1 Hot Spice Mix
- 75g onions, peeled and chopped
- 150g carrots, cut into sticks 1cm x 2cm
- 375g cauliflower, broken into florets
- 150g cabbage, core removed and cut into slices about 2cm wide
- 150g green beans, cut into short slices
- 150g butternut squash, peeled and cut into chunks
- Salt to taste

> **For all the curries REAL ALE LTD RECOMMENDS**
> **Kernel IPA, 7.1%,** the perfect Indian-style beer.

Heat the oil in a large saucepan or wok over a medium heat. Add the spice mix and the onions to the oil and make sure the onions are well coated.

Fry the onions for a few minutes on their own then add the carrots and cauliflower. Stir the curry mix and cook for 5 minutes. Add the cabbage, green beans and the squash. Stir and fry the vegetables for another 5 minutes. Check the salt and add some if you want at this point. Add just enough water to stop the vegetables from sticking to the pan, cover it and simmer the curry for about 10 minutes. You want the vegetables still to have a little crunch in them.

As this is a hot, dry curry a mild dhal or/and a cucumber sambal would complement it, plus boiled rice.

Medium spicy chicken curry

Why not buy one of the delicious home-made mango chutneys from the Crazy Cat's Pantry stall to accompany this classic chicken curry?

Serves 4

- 3 tbs vegetable oil
- 600g onions, peeled and sliced
- 3 cloves of garlic, peeled and chopped fine
- 40g fresh ginger, peeled and chopped fine
- 1 Medium Spice Mix
- 8 chicken pieces (I use thighs and drumsticks)
- 250g full-fat natural yoghurt
- 1 tsp sugar
- Salt to taste
- 1 tbs lime or lemon juice

Heat the oil in a wok or heavy-based pan. Fry the onions, garlic and ginger for about 10 minutes until they are golden and softening. While they are frying, slash the chicken joints with two or three slashes per joint. This will allow the curry spices to add extra flavour to the meat.

Add the curry mix and the chicken joints to the pan. Stir well and fry for 5 minutes. Stir in the yoghurt, a tablespoon at a time, stirring well all the time. Once all the yoghurt is added, add the sugar and, if you need it, sufficient water to just cover the chicken joints. Cover the pan and simmer for 30 minutes or until the chicken is tender.

Check for salt, and add the lime or lemon juice just before you serve the curry with boiled rice.

from Beech Hill Farm

Sarah Edington talks to Chris Savva of Kew Village Market's ever-popular greengrocery stall about apples, potatoes and squashes.

When I first started cooking professionally in the 1970s, most supermarkets offered only four varieties of apple (Bramleys, Golden Delicious, Granny Smiths and Coxes) and only three squashes (marrows, pumpkins and occasionally courgettes). Potatoes were labelled whites or reds. Once a year, in May, we awaited with excitement for the first Jersey Royals, the only named variety, to arrive in the shops. Now, happily, the supermarkets sell far more varieties of apples, squashes and potatoes. But we still don't know how long their journey was from plot to plate, or how they were grown.

Then I talked to Chris Saava whose fruit and vegetables have been delighting Kew shoppers since the market opened. Chris has been growing chemical-free fruit and vegetables for 30 years at Beech Hill Farm. I realised there is another world. A world where fruit and vegetables are grown in their season, where you can trace the short journey of your fruit and vegetables from the field or orchard to your shopping bag.

Chris grows such a huge number of different fruit and vegetables that I had to narrow down our chat. We decided we would look at apples, potatoes and squashes – the first two because they seem so English, both staples of the UK diet, and the third because I wanted to learn more about them. We have eaten cucumbers, pumpkins and marrows from that family for years but many other different squashes are grown at Beech Hill Farm. Chris told me that every variety of his apples, squashes and potatoes is different in size, has a different texture, a different taste, even subtly different colours.

Apples love our climate. They are not a native fruit; they came to Britain with the Romans but now we claim them as our own. Over the centuries generations of growers have crossed our apples to produce different varieties for cooking, for eating, for juicing and not least for making cider. We grow some of the finest apples in the world.

Chris talked about the *Blenheim Orange*. The earliest Blenheims were grown in 1740 by a tailor in Woodstock, a small town which nestles round Blenheim Palace in Oxfordshire. The first Duke of Marlborough won the battle of Blenheim and the palace and the apple are named after that victory. Blenheim Oranges ripen late in September or in early October. They are eating apples with a very distinctive taste: sweet and tangy with a red blush on their greenish-yellowish skin.

Coxes Orange Pippins, first sold commercially in the 1850s, have been favourites for years. In fact, so much so that now you can buy Crimson Coxes, Cherry Coxes, King Coxes and Queen Coxes. Nothing, though, beats biting into a Cox from Chris. Aromatic, sweet and tart at the same time. (By the way, when the word 'orange' is used in the name of an apple variety it has nothing to do with the taste or the colour. It may date back a thousand years or more; the Greeks and the Romans regularly called oranges apples, and the golden apples of Hesperides, which belonged to Zeus, were actually oranges.)

Crispins, apple green and juicy, started on the other side of the world. In Japan an apple called an Ingo was grown in the province of Mutsu. Though tasty, it was prey to pests, so it was crossed with Golden Delicious, a European variety much more resistant to disease. Result? The Crispin, good to eat, cook, juice and keep.

If you are lucky enough to own or inherit an apple tree, here's a final tip from Chris. Question: how do I know an apple is ripe for picking? Answer: wait till the leaves just begin to fall. Then your apples will be perfect.

Squashes originated in the Americas and were taken to other parts of the world by Spanish and Portuguese sailors, and the squash family is now huge and varied. They are all sizes from tiny green courgettes to enormous pumpkins. They are all shapes: *Crown Prince* is oval, *Butternut Squash* is shaped like a church bell, courgettes look like sausages, pumpkins and *Kabochas* are round. Sometimes their name reflects their shape, such as *Green Acorn, Turk's Turban*, and/or their skins' markings or colour – *Red Onion Squash* is a deep rich red, whereas *Harlequin* is multi-coloured. You can eat some squashes raw but generally they lend themselves to all manner of cooking – some make good soup and most take happily to roasting or stir frying.

continued

continued

Chris mentioned the Kabocha Squash as particularly good for cooking. It was introduced to Japan by the Portuguese in the 1540s and now it is grown all over South East Asia. It looks rather like a small knobbly pumpkin with a very dark green skin and the flesh is orange and sweet.

Potatoes also originated in the 'new world' of the Americas. Sir Walter Raleigh is credited with introducing the potato to England in 1588. At first it was a luxury curiosity for the rich but we soon found out that potatoes grew amazingly well in our climate and by the end of the 18th century they were a staple food of the poor. So much so that, when the potato harvest failed three years in a row in Ireland, a million people died and another million emigrated to the United States. Potatoes changed the face of Ireland for ever.

Chris introduced me varieties I had never heard of. *Saxony* potato is considered an old variety, originally from – guess where? – Saxony, which is now a part of modern Germany. With its waxy firm flesh, it is good for salads. *Cara* has a creamy yellow skin with pink eyes, and is good for mashing and baking. *Picasso* is a relative of Cara; the eyes are deeper set and the skin around them a rich red. They are big potatoes, good for baking and roasting.

Baracas are another big potato with a rich caramel-coloured skin, good for roasting and chipping. And there are three cultivars in the Diamond family: *Diamond Ruby* has a deep red skin and is good for steaming, boiling, roasting and baking; *Diamond Russet* has a browner skin and high density flesh, good for large chips; and *Diamond White* is great for thin fries. While we are on the subject of chip and fries, Golden Wonder Crisps are named after *Golden Wonder*, the potato originally used to make them. Trouble was that when the crisps became so successful, the Golden Wonder potatoes could not keep up with the demand, so other varieties are used as well now.

Thanks, Chris, for the information. I shall never look at apples, squashes or potatoes in the same way again!

We are so lucky to have Chris's vegetables and fruits at the market. I've bought the most delicious fruits and vegetables from his stall. Particularly memorable for their flavour: a Savoy cabbage, wonderfully sweet small tomatoes, strawberries and small dark violet plums – all utterly delicious. Then there was the medlar. I'd seen the tree but never the fruit and wondered how did it taste? Absolutely disgusting – if it's October you can try for yourself!

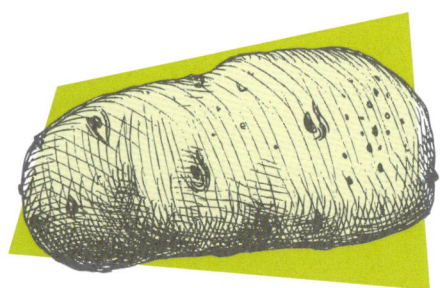

from Belle's Bonbons

'As a child, I remember the sheer pleasure of spending my pocket money on my favourite sweets in the local village shop.' So says Susan Bell, a local Kew confectioner who brings back the fun and enjoyment of traditional sweets in jars as well as the most fabulous fudge. It's a particular pleasure that her daughters Sophie and Amber, who also work on the stall, have contributed a recipe for Rocky Roads, a mixture of chocolate, golden syrup, raisins, biscuits and marshmallows. The most indulgent sweet ever!

Amber & Sophie's rocky roads

Inspired by Nigella Lawson and wickedly delicious!

Makes 24 fingers
125g unsalted butter
200g dark chocolate chips
3 tbs golden syrup
50g raisins
100g rich tea biscuits
100g mini marshmallows
Icing sugar to dust

Put the butter, chocolate and golden syrup in a saucepan over a gentle heat. Stir until the chocolate has melted. Remove from the heat, scoop out about half the mixture and set aside. Stir the raisins into the chocolate mix in the saucepan. Place the biscuits in a plastic bag and crush them with a rolling pin. Stop when you have small pieces – you don't want the biscuits to turn into dust. Fold the biscuit pieces into the mix in the saucepan, then add the marshmallows. Tip the mixture into a 24cm square baking tin and smooth the top. Tip the reserved butter, chocolate and golden syrup mixture over it to make a smooth topping.

Refrigerate for at least 2 hours (preferably longer). To serve, cut it into thin fingers – it's very rich – and dust them with icing sugar.

Coconut ice

Easy to make, good to eat and very pretty.

Makes 12–15 small squares
400g granulated sugar
50ml full-cream milk
150g desiccated coconut
Pink food colouring

Take a shallow 20cm x 13cm tin and either line it with baking paper or brush it with vegetable oil. Place the sugar and milk in a heavy-based saucepan over a low heat and stir carefully until the sugar has dissolved. Bring to the boil and then, on a gentle heat, simmer until a little of the mixture dropped into cold water forms a soft ball between finger and thumb (117C on a sugar thermometer). Remove from the heat and stir in the coconut. Pour half the mixture quickly into the tin. Add a few drops of pink colouring to the other half, stir gently and pour over the first half. Mark into squares and cut when cold. Do not refrigerate.

from Caffè Torelli

Not one of our stalls, of course, but such great supporters of the market from the beginning that we couldn't leave them out of our book!

Caffè Torelli opened in Station Approach in 2010 and was bustling from the beginning. It has a happy clientele of locals, visitors to Kew Gardens and other west Londoners who are lucky enough to find this little piece of Italy in Kew.

Nick Neziri, the manager, is from Sicily. 'In Sicily, we only eat something small at the beginning of the day but although it's small it must be good. So our day starts with an espresso, a glass of water and a cannolo which is always freshly made that day.'

There's a cabinet in Caffè Torelli full of cannoli – small delicious 'biscotti', sweet mouthfuls which originate in Sicily. Here are recipes for two classics. Buon appetito!

Cantucci di prato

These are my own favourite 'biscotti' – crisp sweet rusks studded with toasted almonds, perfect for dunking in coffee. This recipe is adapted from Anna Del Conte's wonderful Gastronomy of Italy.

Makes about 40

- 100g flaked almonds
- 40g pine nuts
- 250g superfine plain flour
- 225g caster sugar
- ½ tsp baking powder
- 3 eggs
- 1 tsp fennel seeds

Preheat the oven to 200C/fan 180/gas 6

Put the almonds and pine nuts on a tin and bake them for 5 minutes in the preheated oven. Remove from the oven and set aside.

Sift the flour, sugar and baking powder onto the work surface. Make a well in the centre. Beat the eggs and the fennel seeds until thick and creamy. Pour the mixture into the well and work it gradually into the dry ingredients, adding the toasted nuts at the end. When everything is well mixed, divide it in half and pat and roll each piece into a 30cm sausage. Lay them well apart on a baking sheet, lined with baking paper and bake in the oven for 15–18 minutes.

Take the tray out of the oven and reduce the temperature to *140C/fan 120/gas 1.*

Cool the cantucci for 10 minutes then cut them diagonally in 1cm slices. Lay the slices side by side on the tray and return them to the oven for the second baking – about 45 minutes, by which time they should be well dried out.

Cool completely before storing in an airtight tin where they will keep for 2–3 months. You get a lot of cantucci from this recipe – but they make really good presents!

Cannoli siciliana

To make these authentic cannoli, horn moulds or cannoli tubes are needed – you can get them easily on the Internet.

Makes around 20

- 250g plain flour
- 1 tsp cocoa powder
- 1 tsp coffee, freshly ground
- 30g butter, cut into small dice and softened
- 25g caster sugar
- 60ml white wine
- 1 egg, beaten
- Olive oil for deep frying
- Icing sugar to dust

To make the pastry, sift the flour, cocoa powder, coffee and sugar in a large bowl, add the butter and mix well together. Gradually add the wine until the mixture forms a pastry dough. Form it into a ball, wrap it in clingfilm and leave it to rest in the fridge for an hour. While it is resting, make one of the suggested fillings.

To make the cannoli shells, lightly flour a clean work surface and roll out the pastry to a thickness of about 3mm. With a round 7.5cm cutter, cut circles from the pastry and wrap them around the moulds, securing the edges with the beaten egg.

Heat the olive oil in a large pan to 180C. Fry the cannoli until golden brown. Drain on kitchen paper, then gently remove the moulds. When the cannoli are cool, fill them with the ricotta or ganache filling. Sprinkle with icing sugar and serve.

FILLING 1

- 400g ricotta cheese
- 150g icing sugar
- 25g chocolate chips
- 50g candied fruits, finely chopped

FILLING 2

- 225g dark chocolate chips
- 200ml double cream
- 1 tbs dark rum (optional)

Ricotta, chocolate chip and candied fruit

Place the ricotta and icing sugar in a large bowl and whisk until creamy. Fold in the chocolate chips and candied fruits.

Chocolate ganache

Place the chocolate chips in a bowl large enough to take all the ingredients. Bring the cream slowly up to the boil in a small saucepan. Watch very carefully – you don't want it to boil over. Tip the hot cream over the chips and whisk until it is smooth. You can stir in a tablespoon of rum at this point. Leave the ganache to cool.

from Carolyn Dawson

Carolyn Dawson has been a chef for over 25 years and at the market she sells dishes made from seasonal ingredients lovingly cooked by her at home in Kew. Her stall is besieged every market day by eager customers opting out of cooking Sunday lunch – the smell of the soups, the stunning-looking salads and the terrific tarts all entice the hungry shopper. Here are Carolyn's recipes for two of her signature salads, two soups, two slices and two tarts.

Spicy lentil, cauliflower & butternut squash salad with coriander

Warm, spicy flavours for any time of the year – delicious served just on its own or with some meat or fish.

Serves 8–10

1 small bunch of coriander
1 medium onion, peeled and chopped
2.5cm piece of fresh ginger, peeled and sliced
1 or 2 chillies, deseeded
4 cloves of garlic, peeled
3 tbs sunflower oil
1 tsp mustard seeds
½ tsp each of ground coriander, cumin, turmeric and paprika
300g Puy lentils
200g tin of chopped tomatoes
1 tsp sugar
400g peeled and diced butternut squash
400g cauliflower florets
Salt and pepper

Preheat the oven to 180C/fan 160/gas 4.

Pick the coriander leaves off the stalks and set aside in the fridge. Put the coriander stalks, onion, ginger, chilli and garlic into a food processor and pulse until you have a rough purée. Heat the oil in a heavy-based pot, add the mustard seeds and fry until they pop. Quickly add the onion mix to the pan and stir over a low heat for about 5–10 minutes until it's very soft and has a little colour. Add the dry spices and fry for another 5 minutes. Add the tinned tomatoes, sugar and lentils to the spice mix, cover with water and simmer for approximately 15–20 minutes. The lentils should be cooked by then – test them and give them a few more minutes if they feel a little hard still. Let the lentils cool while you prepare the squash and cauliflower.

Spread the diced squash on a tray and drizzle with olive oil, salt and pepper. Roast in the preheated oven for about 15–20 minutes until soft but still holding their shape. Place the cauliflower into a pan of boiling water for 3–4 minutes, drain and let cool. When all the different components are cooled, mix all gently together with most of the picked coriander and season to taste. Pile it all into a salad bowl and top with the remaining coriander leaves.

Two slices

These slices are a wonderful idea – the only problem is which topping to choose. And note the pastry – totally different from the usual shortcrust but, as Carolyn says, 'It tastes good, it's very forgiving and easy to use, and always delivers a crisp base.' A real recommendation!

Each slice will feed 6–8

For the pastry
350g plain flour
A pinch of salt
125g chilled and diced butter
2 eggs
100ml warm water
1 tsp dried yeast or 2 tsp fresh yeast
1 tsp sugar

Place the flour, salt and butter in a food processor and switch on until the mixture resembles fine breadcrumbs. Mix together the warm water, yeast and sugar and leave a few minutes to activate. (This is when it bubbles and fizzes a little.) Tip the flour and butter mix into a wide bowl and make a well in the centre.

Whisk the eggs together and pour into the well with the yeast mix. Bring it all together with your hands, then tip it out onto a floured work surface and knead to a smooth dough, adding more flour if it is still a bit sticky. Place it into a bowl, cover with cling film and leave to prove for at least 30 minutes in a warm place. Then chill it in the fridge for an hour to firm it up and make it easier to roll out.

Roll out the pastry to about 1cm thickness to fit a shallow 25cm x 35cm tray lined with baking parchment. Trim the edges and set it aside to rest while the toppings are prepared.

TOPPING 1
1 tbs olive oil
2 red onions, peeled
200g blue cheese (Stilton or Gorgonza are both fine)
6 figs, halved
Chopped walnuts and rocket leaves, to serve

Preheat the oven to 180C/ fan 160/gas 4.

TOPPING 2
1 large onion, sliced and cooked soft over a low heat
200g cooked and sliced new potatoes
150g sliced pancetta
1 small round of Reblochon cheese, about 200g, sliced
Salt and pepper

Preheat the oven to 180C/ fan 160/gas 4.

Red onion, blue cheese & fig with rocket & walnuts
Slice the onions, drizzle with a little olive oil, salt and pepper and roast in the oven for approximately 15 minutes, until softened. When they're cool spread them over the prepared pastry, leaving 1cm edge all round, crumble over the blue cheese and then place the figs over the cheese. Bake in the oven for 15–20 minutes until the pastry is crisp on the bottom and cheese is melted. When the slice has cooled a little, top it with chopped walnuts and scatter over some rocket leaves and cracked black pepper.

Potato, Reblochon cheese & pancetta
Spread the sliced softened onions over the prepared pastry, leaving 1cm edge all round, scatter the potato slices and season with the salt and pepper. Lay the pancetta slices on top and finally the slices of cheese. Bake in the oven for 15–20 minutes until golden, crisp and melting.

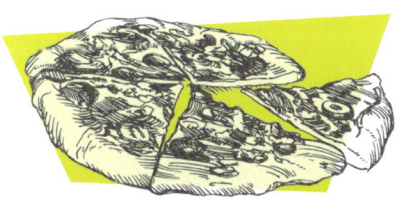

Two tarts

Carolyn's savoury tarts are always much in demand – not least by visitors heading for a picnic in Kew Gardens.

Each tart serves 6–8

For both tarts preheat the oven to 180C/fan 160/gas 4.

> **THE GOOD WINE SHOP RECOMMENDS**
> **Domaine Bruno Sorg, Pinot Gris, Alsace.**
> The grape that we know as Pinot Grigio in its crisp dry incarnation in the north of Italy produces very different results in the warmth of Alsace, giving wines with much richer fruit, a hint of honey and a creamy mouth-feel.

Using the yeast pastry described on the previous page, grease and line a 26cm fluted tart tin with a removable bottom or 6–8 individual tart tins. Trim up the edges and chill while the fillings are prepared.

FILLING 1

- 250g ham, diced or shredded
- 2 leeks, diced and sautéed in a little butter and olive oil until soft
- 150g grated cheddar
- 1 tsp chopped parsley
- 4 eggs
- 600ml single cream
- Salt and pepper

FILLING 2

- 1 butternut squash, peeled, diced and roasted soft
- 150g of feta cheese, crumbled
- A handful of pitted black olives
- 1 tsp chopped fresh or dry oregano
- 4 eggs
- 600ml single cream
- Salt and pepper

Ham, cheese & leek

Fill the prepared tart base with the ham, leek and grated cheddar. Sprinkle over the chopped parsley. Whisk the eggs and cream together and season with salt and pepper to taste (remembering that the ham and cheese will be slightly salty). Pour this into the tart to just under the top – take care not to overfill it as the pastry will expand a little when baking. Place on a tray and bake in the oven for about 20 minutes. The tart should be firm but retaining a slight wobble and the pastry crisp and golden.

Pumpkin, feta, olive & oregano

Place the squash, feta and olives in the prepared tart tin. Sprinkle over the oregano. Whisk the eggs and cream together and season with salt and pepper to taste. Pour this into the tart to just under the top – take care not to overfill it as the pastry will expand a little when baking. Place on a tray and bake in the oven for about 20 minutes. The tart should be firm but retaining a slight wobble and the pastry crisp and golden.

Lamb, vegetable & pot barley soup

Pot barley is an old-fashioned pulse much used by frugal cooks. It has a natural affinity with lamb and is a welcome nutty addition to this robust broth. You can buy it in Oliver's Wholefood Store.

Serves 8

1 lamb shank
2 tbs olive or vegetable oil
1 medium onion, peeled and diced
1 peeled carrot, 1 stick of celery, 1 trimmed leek, all diced
1 parsnip, ½ a celeriac, 150g swede, all peeled and diced also
2 bay leaves
1 tsp fresh thyme leaves
1 chicken or lamb stock cube
150g pot barley
Salt and pepper
Chopped fresh parsley to garnish

Seal the lamb shank in a little of the oil until nicely browned all over. Set aside while you partly cook the vegetables. Warm the rest of the oil in a large pan and add the onion, carrot, celery and leek. Cook over a low heat until they begin to soften. Add the remaining vegetables, bay leaves and thyme and cook for another 5 minutes, stirring occasionally. Add the lamb shank, stock cube and enough water to cover it all well. Simmer for about an hour until the lamb is soft and falling off the bone.

Remove the lamb shank and leave to cool. You may need to add some more water if the soup has reduced too much. Place the barley in another pan and cover with cold water. Bring to the boil, simmer for 25 minutes, drain and rinse under a running tap. (This will rid the barley of extra starch so the soup will not be cloudy.) Add the drained barley to the soup, pick the meat off the shank, chop and return it to the pan. Bring the soup back to the boil, adding more stock or water if it's a little thick and season well. Finish with the chopped parsley.

Sweet potato, chilli, ginger & coconut soup

A blend of tastes, exotic and homely, in a creamy spicy soup.

Serves 6–8

2 tbs vegetable oil
1 medium onion, peeled and chopped
1 leek, trimmed and chopped
1 stick of celery, chopped
4 cloves of garlic, peeled
1 or 2 chillies, deseeded and chopped
2.5cm piece of fresh ginger, peeled and chopped
1kg sweet potato, peeled and chopped
1 vegetable stock cube, dissolved in 1 litre water
400g tin of coconut milk
Salt and pepper
Chopped fresh coriander to garnish

Heat the oil in a large pan and cook the onion, leek, celery, garlic, chilli and ginger over a low heat until soft but not coloured. Add the sweet potatoes and stock, adding more water if the ingredients are not covered. Bring to the boil, turn the heat down to a simmer and cook for 20–30 minutes until all the vegetables are soft. Purée in a blender until smooth, return to the pan with the coconut milk, reheat gently and season well with salt and pepper. Serve with chopped fresh coriander on top.

> **THE GOOD WINE SHOP RECOMMENDS**
> **Framingham Classic Riesling, Marlborough, New Zealand.**
> This is Riesling produced with great love and care. The heady nose is all blossom and juicy citrus, and the flavours are orange, peach, ginger and lemon peel.

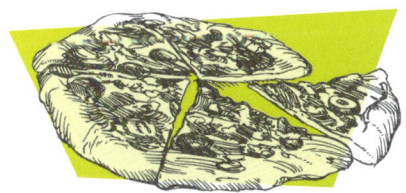

Garden vegetable salad with salsa verde

Make this in the spring when the new season's green vegetables and herbs appear in the shops. Or in the winter you can make it with frozen vegetables and give yourself a taste of spring to banish the winter blues.

Serves 6

- 200g new potatoes
- 120g fresh or frozen peas
- 120g fresh or frozen broad beans
- 100g green beans, topped and tailed and cut in half
- 1 courgette, cut into 1cm dice
- 5 asparagus spears, sliced on an angle

For the salsa verde

- 150ml olive oil
- 1 clove of garlic, peeled
- 4 tbs parsley leaves
- 4 tbs mint leaves
- 2 tbs basil
- 1 tsp wholegrain mustard
- 1 tsp drained capers
- 1 tbs drained and chopped cornichons
- Salt and pepper to taste

Boil the potatoes, drain when cooked, cool and slice. Bring a pan of water to the boil, place the beans in it for a minute or two then scoop them out into iced water to cool. (This will help them to keep their colour.) Repeat this process with the peas, courgette, broad beans and asparagus. Drain all the vegetables well, then put them into a large bowl and mix gently with the new potatoes.

To make the salsa verde, place the oil, garlic and herbs in a blender and blend until smooth. Transfer the sauce to a bowl and stir in the mustard, capers, cornichons and salt and pepper. Gently add enough sauce to coat the vegetables and serve.

Any excess salsa verde is great to serve with roast chicken, beef or cold meats.

> **THE GOOD WINE SHOP RECOMMENDS**
> **Amedeo Custoza Superiore DOC 2012, Cavalchina.**
> An excellent blend of Cortese and Garganega (the grapes for Gavi and Soave respectively), this deftly balanced white wine has a velvety texture with plenty of crisp citrus and stone fruit. Partial ageing in oak casks adds breadth and richness as well as some honey and vanilla on the finish.

from Crazy Cat's Pantry

Carol Watfa cooks up chutneys, preserves, relishes and marinades. She's passionate about food and inspirational in her unusual recipes. The vegetables she uses are organic and everything is hand made at her home in Barnes. Carol is a whizz at unusual blends of fruit, vegetables, herbs and spices – look up her website www.crazycatspantry.com for the full range of her preserves.

She's given us two chutney recipes, both for foods which are grown easily and love our climate. There is often a glut of rhubarb and beetroot during particular times of year. Never turn down an offer of either now! Roo Chutney and Beat Chutney taste wonderful and keep for a long time.

Nothing beats a hunk of bread, a slice of cheese and a spoonful of one of Carol's specials!

Carol's tips for perfect preserves

Here Carole takes you through the preparation of fruit or vegetables, tips on sterilising equipment and the process itself. It is quite straightforward but it puts the mind at rest for the novice.

Equipment

You'll need jars, a funnel and a large thick-bottomed stainless steel pan. In this day and age, most lids are vinegar- and acid-proof but do check and buy new ones if necessary.

Half an hour before your chutney or jam is about to alchemise into something amazing, clean the jars in seriously hot soapy water, rinse well and place upside down on a baking tray. Turn the oven on to *100C/fan 100/gas ¼* and leave the jars there until they're ready to be filled. Wash and rinse the lids well, then put them in a bowl, covered in boiling water, til you're ready to bottle.

Produce

Place the vegetables and/or fruit in a spotlessly clean sink, fill up with water and pour in a cup of distilled malt vinegar so that any residual pesticides are less likely to stay attached. After 10 or 15 minutes, drain the sink and give your produce a good rinsing off before laying it flat on clean tea towels to let it dry before continuing with the recipe.

Potting up

When your chutney is ready, place the hot jars on a tea towel and pour in the chutney/jam through the funnel, leaving 1 cm of space from the top of the jar. Please remember that chutneys shrink over time so fill the jars a little bit more. Make sure that no bubbles appear in the jar as they may be the breeding ground of some undesirable bacteria (push a clean non-scratchy knife into the sides to make the holes disappear). Pick a clean lid, dry it well, then secure it over the jar top.

Bottling procedures (optional)

There are three main ones: slow water-bath method, fast water-bath method and pressure cooker. If you're going to be producing jars to sell to the public you should really spend a lot of time researching the subject and adopting whichever method appeals to you. If, however, you are doing chutneys, jams and marmalades for yourself, family and friends, as long as you adopt a seriously hygienic approach to handling fruit and vegetable, you should be fine.

Inspiration

Don't be afraid of what your palate dictates. As you get more comfortable with this form of food preservation, you will definitely want to experiment. My tastes are quite rebellious – for instance, I usually use as little sugar as I can get away with because, even though I choose the healthiest option (unrefined cane sugar), it is still sugar. Also, my taste buds do not like 'bland', so I tend to up the spice volume a little.

'Spicy Roo' was concocted because I had some rhubarb left over from other popular Crazy Cat's Pantry recipes, so I took all my spices out and decided on which would go with it. And I made 'Beat-root' with beets that were roasted and not boiled as original recipe suggested and certainly not with the type of vinegar advised… Good luck and keep exploring and preserving!

Beat-root chutney

This beetroot chutney recipe is loosely based on one from www.recipesatrandom.com. It's quite powerful so it goes really well with bland cheeses and white meats. The pepper and spices should all be freshly ground.

Makes around 5–6 jars (350g each)

- 1kg beetroot, organic if possible
- 1 medium cooking apple, peeled, cored and cut into cubes
- 1 large onion, peeled and sliced
- ½ litre red wine vinegar
- 250g unrefined cane sugar
- 50g large raisins
- 2 tbs chopped fresh ginger
- 3 tsp white pepper
- 1 tbs allspice
- ½ tbs cloves

Preheat the oven to 180C/fan 160/gas 4.

Roast the beetroots whole in foil in the oven for just over an hour. Once they've cooled, take the skin off and chop the beetroot into little cubes. Put in a preserving pan, or any thick-bottomed stainless steel pan large enough to contain all the ingredients and with space for the chutney to bubble. Add the rest of the ingredients.

This one is a slow cook, so take your time. Simmer for a couple of hours until the consistency feels right, then bottle.

This chutney should keep for at least one year if unopened. The longer you wait for it, the nicer it tastes. Needless to say that once it's opened, keep it in the fridge.

Spicy roo chutney

Rhubarb chutney – a spicy assault on the senses. For the best result, the peppers and all the spices should be freshly ground.

Makes around 5–6 jars (350g each)

1.5kg rhubarb, de-stringed
500ml cider vinegar
500g unrefined cane sugar
75g jalapeño chilli peppers, deseeded and diced
75g large raisins
50g garlic, peeled and crushed
2 tsp cinnamon
2 tsp ground cloves
½ tsp allspice
A good grind of black pepper
1 tsp chilli flakes (freshly ground from home-dried chillis if possible)
1 tsp sea salt

Cut the rhubarb stems into little chunks and put in the preserving pan (or any stainless-steel thick-bottomed pan large enough to contain all the ingredients and allow space for them to bubble). Add all other ingredients on top, mix well, and put on a low heat for a couple of hours.

Grab a book, and remember that patience is a virtue – also stir from time to time. By then, the rhubarb will gave softened considerably and all elements have had time to get to know each other. Turn the heat up if you feel there's too much liquid and contents have not thickened up enough. If that's the case, stir vigorously until desired consistency – but remembering that chutneys thicken when they are cool. Turn the heat off and bottle.

Don't open the jar for at least a month. If properly bottled, the chutney should keep for two years unopened in a dark cool place, but refrigerate it after opening.

from La Crêpe Des Delices

Djamel Cheurfa comes from Lyon – sometimes titled the food capital of France. A trained chef, he makes and sells the most delicious savoury galettes and sweet crêpes from his bright blue Citroën van. (Djamel's mobile crêperie can attend parties and school fairs as well as appearing regularly at the market – see www.lacrepedesdelices for the details.)

Here he gives us one of his savoury batter recipes, complete with filling, and takes us through the perfect sweet pancake and two fillings, one the original Crêpes Suzettes and the other deliciously fruity. Djamel is also sharing with us a sophisticated version of Pain Perdu and his own recipe for that classic of French cuisine Boeuf Bouguignon.

Savoury crêpes (galettes de sarazin)

This galette recipe uses gluten-free flour which is very tasty and perfect for making the most incredible savoury crêpes. You can find it in Oliver's Wholefood Store or in some supermarkets such as Waitrose.

Makes 15 galettes
- 250g sarazin (buckwheat) flour
- 1 egg
- 350ml water
- 50g butter, melted
- A pinch of salt
- 350ml milk
- A knob of butter

Put the flour in a large mixing bowl and make a hole in the middle. Add the egg, butter, salt, and the water. Mix until the batter becomes smooth and then add the milk a little at a time. (It's easiest to make with a hand mixer or food processor.) Rest the batter for at least 1 hour in the fridge – overnight is even better.

Warm a knob of butter in your frying pan (ideally non-stick) and when it is melted add a large spoonful of the galette batter. When the galette is cooked on one side, turn it over and gently warm the other side. Now it is time to assemble the galettes and filling!

For each galette
- 3 slices of goat's cheese
- 1 tbs of chopped walnuts
- Clear honey to drizzle

Goat's cheese, walnut & honey filling
Slice the goat's cheese on to the galette with a scattering walnuts and a drizzle of honey. Then fold the galette and slide it onto a plate. *Voilà!* You have a delicious goat's cheese galette!

> **THE GOOD WINE SHOP RECOMMENDS**
> **Badenhorst, Secateurs Chenin Blanc, Coastal Region, South Africa.** Flavours of apple and honey and a creamy texture give the wine richness and weight while retaining the brilliantly zippy tang of Chenin's acid backbone.

Sweet crêpes

Here are Djamel's secrets for making perfect sweet crêpes – Pancake Day was never like this!

Makes 15 crêpes

250g plain flour, sifted

A small pinch of salt

3 eggs, lightly beaten

70g caster sugar

500ml milk

1 tbs honey

A few drops of vanilla essence

Put the flour and salt into a large mixing bowl and make a well in the middle. Add the eggs, caster sugar and a small amount of milk. Mix slowly so that all ingredients are combined, then add the rest of the milk a little bit at a time. Finally add the honey and vanilla essence. Beat until the batter is smooth. Now rest the batter for at least an hour – overnight is best.

Turn the oven on so that it is just warm *(100C/fan 100/gas ¼)* and put in a dinner plate. You are now ready to make your first crêpe. Heat a non-stick frying pan, put in a small knob of butter and swirl it around. Drop a tablespoon of the batter into the pan, spread it around and cook the first side until it is golden brown. Flip the crêpe over, using a pallet knife or your flipping skills!

Keep the crêpes warm in the oven until you want to fill them. Interleave them on the plate with strips of baking paper – that way they won't stick to each other.

Both the filling recipes will fill two crêpes which constitute a helping for one person. Just multiply the quantities for the number of lucky diners.

FILLING 1

6 strawberries, sliced

2 tbs chocolate pieces

Cinnamon

FILLING 2

40g unsalted butter

40g sugar

2 tbs Grand Marnier

Fruity filling

Spread the crêpes with the strawberries and the chocolate pieces. Roll the crêpes and finish with a dusting of cinnamon.

Crêpes Suzettes filling

First melt the butter, then add the sugar and the Grand Marnier. Either pour this over the folded crêpes as it is or, if you are brave, heat the liquid until it is very hot, light it with a match so that it is flaming and pour it directly over the crêpes to serve in the classic dramatic style.

Smoked salmon pain perdu & salad

An elegant, indulgent brunch or light supper.

Serves 2

- 20g butter
- 1 tbs olive oil
- 2 eggs
- 1 tbs chopped parsley
- Salt and pepper
- 2 thick slices of wholemeal bread
- 100g smoked salmon
- 1 tsp sesame seeds, to serve

For the salad

- 100g mixed leaves, washed and ready to serve
- 25g pine nuts
- 1 carrot, peeled and chopped into fine batons
- 1 tbs olive oil
- 1 tsp balsamic vinegar
- ½ tsp Dijon mustard

Melt the butter and oil in a frying pan and, while the mix is heating, beat the eggs and parsley together and season with salt and pepper. Remember that the smoked salmon is salty, so go easy on the salt. When the butter/oil in the frying pan is golden brown, it is ready to receive the bread slices.

Dip each slice of bread in the egg mixture, place in the frying pan and cook both sides until they are both golden brown. Take off the heat, take out the slices. Pat them with kitchen roll to absorb any excess fat and slice each of them into three oblong pieces. Cool on a wire rack.

While the bread is cooling, make the salad. Put the leaves, pine nuts and carrots in a bowl. Mix together the oil, vinegar and mustard together, pour over the salad and mix gently. To serve, place half the salad on each plate. Roll the smoked salmon around each bread piece, lay gently on the top of the salad and sprinkle sesame seeds over the top.

> **THE GOOD WINE SHOP RECOMMENDS**
> **Reyneke Sauvignon Blanc, Stellenbosch, South Africa.**
> A smooth, almost creamy Sauvignon that still has enough bite to cut through the oiliness of the fish.

Boeuf bourguignon

'I would like to introduce you one of my favourite dishes, Boeuf Bourguignon. Although it takes a long time to cook it is surprisingly easy to make and the end result is just amazing.'

Serves 4–6

- 1kg casserole steak cut into 5cm pieces
- 1 bouquet garni (2 bay leaves, 5 sprigs parsley, 4 sprigs of thyme)
- 75cl red wine
- 2 tbs olive oil
- 30g butter
- 3 carrots, peeled and chopped into batons
- 2 onions, peeled and sliced
- 250g button mushrooms
- 1 tbs plain flour
- 3 cloves of garlic, peeled
- Salt and pepper
- 2 sprigs of parsley to serve

The night before (or at least 5 hours before starting to cook) rinse the bouquet garni herbs and chop the thyme and parsley. Put the meat into a large dish, season with salt, then pour over the wine and add the herbs. Cover the dish and place in the fridge to marinate.

Once the meat is marinated, heat the oil and butter in a large oven-proof casserole over a high heat. Remove the beef from the marinade (being sure to keep all the liquid for later) and add it to the casserole dish. Keep moving the beef around so all sides get browned equally.

Add the carrots, onions and mushrooms and then sprinkle the flour on top. Stir until the flour gets a golden colour. Add the red wine and herbs marinade and bring to the boil, stirring continuously. Crush the garlic cloves into the casserole and add salt and pepper to taste. Cover and leave over very low heat for at least 2½ hours, making sure you check the pan and give it a stir every 30 minutes so ingredients don't stick to the bottom. Alternatively you can cook the boeuf in the oven (*preheated to 140C, fan 120, gas 1*). If your sauce stays too liquid, leave the pan uncovered for a while.

The beef is ready once it is soft. Check the seasoning and garnish the dish with the fresh parsley. A beef casserole is always tastier the day after you have made it, so if you've got the patience to wait until tomorrow you will experience an even better flavour!

> **THE GOOD WINE SHOP RECOMMENDS**
> **Chorey-les-Beaunes, Domaine Tollot-Beaut, France.**
> A red Burgundy is a must, and Tollot-Beaut produce a first-class Chorey with typically rich, ripe, round forest berry flavours with a long, taut, pure finish.

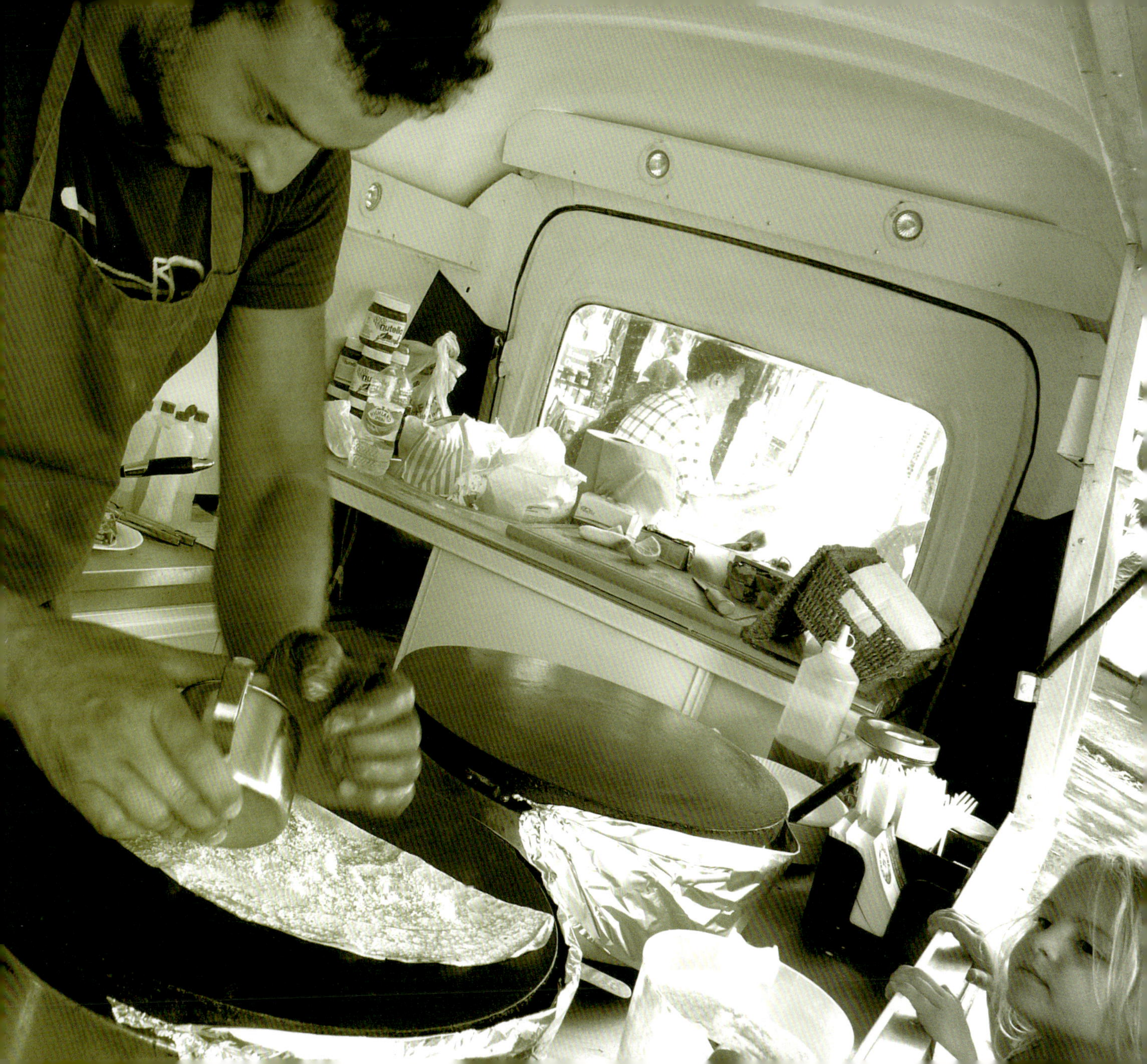
nutella

from Fidelma's Kitchen

Fidelma Charalambous has studied at the best cookery school in Ireland and eaten the best cookies in California. Now she cooks them for us to buy at her stall at the market. The result is scrumptious goodies that are irresistible to children and grown-ups alike.

Fidelma's cookie mix is a closely-guarded secret, but here are three recipes made with her cookies.

By the way, Fidelma sells nicely presented Cookie Mix Kits with delicious add-ons like chocolate chips, raisins, nuts... Simple to make and so rewarding – a great gift for a child who likes cooking or an adult with a sweet tooth.

Cookie-crumb ice-cream pops

These are great for children's parties and, if you can stand the mess, kids love making them too. However, you must start this recipe at least four hours before you need the pops – better still if the ice-cream can be made the night before.

Makes 30

- 300ml whipping cream
- 50g caster sugar
- Juice and grated rind of 2 large oranges
- 200g melted chocolate
- 6–8 cookies, crushed (you should end up with a weight of 450g crumbs)
- 30 ice-cream sticks

First, make and freeze the ice-cream. Whisk the cream until it forms soft peaks, then fold in the sugar and the orange juice and grated rind. Put into a plastic container and freeze. To avoid big crystals, after a couple of hours remove the ice-cream from the freezer and beat it again until the mixture becomes too solid to continue.

Take a tray large enough to take 30 pops and line it with cling film. (If this size is too big for your freezer, then use two smaller ones.) As quickly as you can, create small balls of ice-cream, using a melon baller or two teaspoons. Place the balls on the tray(s) and return to the freezer to firm up.

While the balls are freezing, melt the chocolate either in a bowl set over boiling water or in the microwave. Leave it to cool a bit but it must not start to solidify again. Crush the cookies in the food processor or pop them in a plastic bag and bash with a rolling pin.

Have the sticks, the melted chocolate and the crushed cookies all to hand. You are going to have to work fast. Take the tray from the freezer. Push an ice-cream stick in each ball. Holding the stick, quickly dunk the ball first in the chocolate and then in the crumbs and return it to the tray. Once they're all done, place the tray back in the freezer to firm up again before serving.

Millionaire cookie bars

Here's another idea for cookie lovers. You can't make a more decadently delicious bar – it's the one that millionaires keep in their biscuit tins, hence its name!

Makes 16

For the base
300g hazelnut chocolate-chip cookies
50g butter

For the caramel filling
400g tin condensed milk
75g butter
75g soft light brown sugar
100g toasted hazelnuts

For the topping
1 tbs sunflower or light olive oil
200g dark chocolate

Preheat the oven to 160C/ fan 140/gas 3.

Line a 20cm square tin with non-stick baking paper. For the base, break the cookies into chunks and crisp them up for 10 minutes in the oven – keep an eye on them because they burn easily. Allow them to cool. Then make them into crumbs, either in a food processor or put them in a plastic bag and bash them with a rolling pin. Melt the butter gently in a saucepan, mix in the crumbled cookies and press the mixture down evenly across the base of the prepared tin. Leave in the fridge to set.

For the filling, either put the condensed milk, butter and sugar in a saucepan and cook gently over a low heat, stirring all the time, or put all the ingredients in a microwaveable bowl and heat on full power about 7–9 minutes. You must keep stirring the mixture, all the time if you are using a saucepan and once a minute if you are using the microwave. The filling is ready when it turns thick and fudge-coloured. Be very careful – the mix does become very hot. Pour the filling into the tin and spread it evenly over the cookie base.

Scatter the hazelnuts over the mixture. Then melt the chocolate gently with the oil, either in a bowl set in a saucepan of boiling water or in the microwave. Pour it over the caramel filling and shake the tin from side to side to allow the chocolate to cover the entire surface. Leave to set. To serve, cut into squares.

Tiramisu

Fidelma says, 'Make this delicious dessert for a party in a big bowl or for a picnic in individual portions in jam jars.' I loved this second idea. What a fantastic climax to an alfresco meal!

Serves 4–6
3 tbs instant coffee, dissolved in 100ml boiling water
2 tbs rum or brandy
250g mascarpone, at room temperature
250g soft cream cheese, at room temperature
125g icing sugar
2 large double-chocolate-chip cookies
6 large coffee cookies

Make up the coffee, allow it to cool and add the brandy or rum. Beat the mascarpone with the cream cheese and icing sugar until all are blended well together.

Crumble the chocolate-chip cookies. If you are doing this in a food processor, be careful. You don't want them to crumble into dust. If you haven't got a processor, then put the cookies in a plastic bag and bash them with a rolling pin.

Break the coffee cookies into chunks and arrange half of them in the bottom of a glass bowl big enough to take all the ingredients, or in individual glasses or jars. Pour over some of the coffee mixture, allowing it to soak into the cookies. Layer on half the mascarpone mixture. Sprinkle that layer with half the chocolate crumbs. Then repeat the process, finishing up with chocolate crumbs. Either cover the bowl with cling film or the jars with lids and leave overnight in the fridge.

from Flax Farm

Clare Skelton grows linseed lovingly at Flax Farm in Sussex. The crop is grown in an environmentally friendly and sustainable way, ensuring that there is still a rich diversity of wildlife on the farm. A range of products are derived from the top-quality linseed (also known as flaxseed), nature's richest sustainable source of Omega 3. Golden and bronze linseeds are cold-ground to produce fibre-rich meal or cold-pressed for smooth, mild-tasting oil. On Clare's stall you will find both meal and oil for sale and advice on how to introduce this wonder food into your diet.

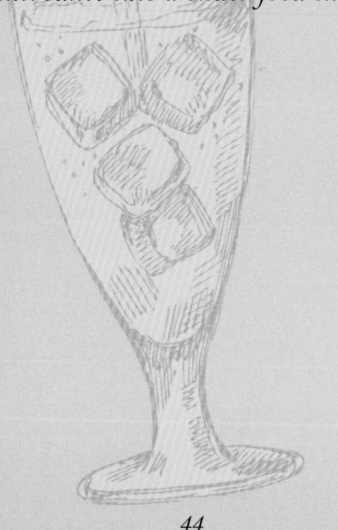

Flax farm flapjacks

Here's the recipe for the delicious Flaxjacks that Clare sells on her stall.

Makes 14–16

- 250g butter
- 70ml syrup
- 200g unrefined brown sugar
- 280g oats
- 187g freshly ground golden or bronze linseed meal

Preheat the oven to 150C/fan 130/gas 2.

Gently warm and melt the butter with the syrup. (The easiest way to measure syrup is to warm it gently. It will thin and you will be able to pour the required measurement.) When they are both combined, add the sugar, oats and linseed meal. Line a 30cm x 20cm baking tray with baking paper. Press the flapjack mixture into the tin, level off the top and bake for approximately 20 minutes. The flapjacks are ready when the top has a skin and is lightly browned. Cool in the tin and cut into oblong biscuits.

Fruit & linseed salad

This can be served as either a breakfast salad or a dessert – it'll feed at least four. Add the linseed cream below for a lovely contrast topping.

- 2 kiwis, peeled, cut in half and sliced
- 1 mango, peeled and diced
- 2 thick slices of pineapple, peeled and chopped
- 2 slices of melon, peeled and chopped
- 2 pears, peeled and chopped
- Any of the berries – strawberries, raspberries, blueberries – taste delicious and provide a contrast in colour
- 2–4 heaped tbs fresh linseed meal

Put all the prepared fruit and their juice in a bowl. If you want to make the salad some time before you serve it, cover the prepared fruit with clingfilm and chill it. Stir in the ground linseed meal at the last minute and serve immediately. The ground linseed 'dissolves' into the juice of the fruit!

Linseed cream

Dr Johanna Budwig invented the Budwig Diet to maintain a healthy lifestyle. This is her recipe.

- 180g cold-pressed linseed (flaxseed) oil
- 400g fat-free Quark cottage cheese
- A little raw honey or sweetener of choice
- Chopped nuts to serve

Place the three ingredients in a bowl. Blitz thoroughly with a hand blender and use to top the fruit and linseed salad. Sprinkle with chopped nuts.

Flax super smoothie

This could be the easiest, healthiest breakfast ever!

Serves 2
- 1 banana
- Either a peach or hulled strawberries
- 25g fresh linseed meal
- 2 tsp cold-pressed linseed oil
- Fruit juice, milk or yoghourt to make up to 500ml

Simply liquidise all of these ingredients for a super-healthy and delicious meal in a glass.

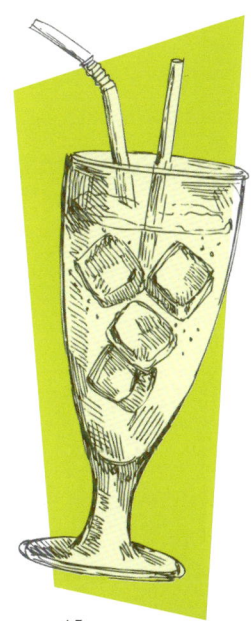

Waterloo
£26.50/Kg

Vegetable
Samosa
£1

Chocolate Orange
Raspberry

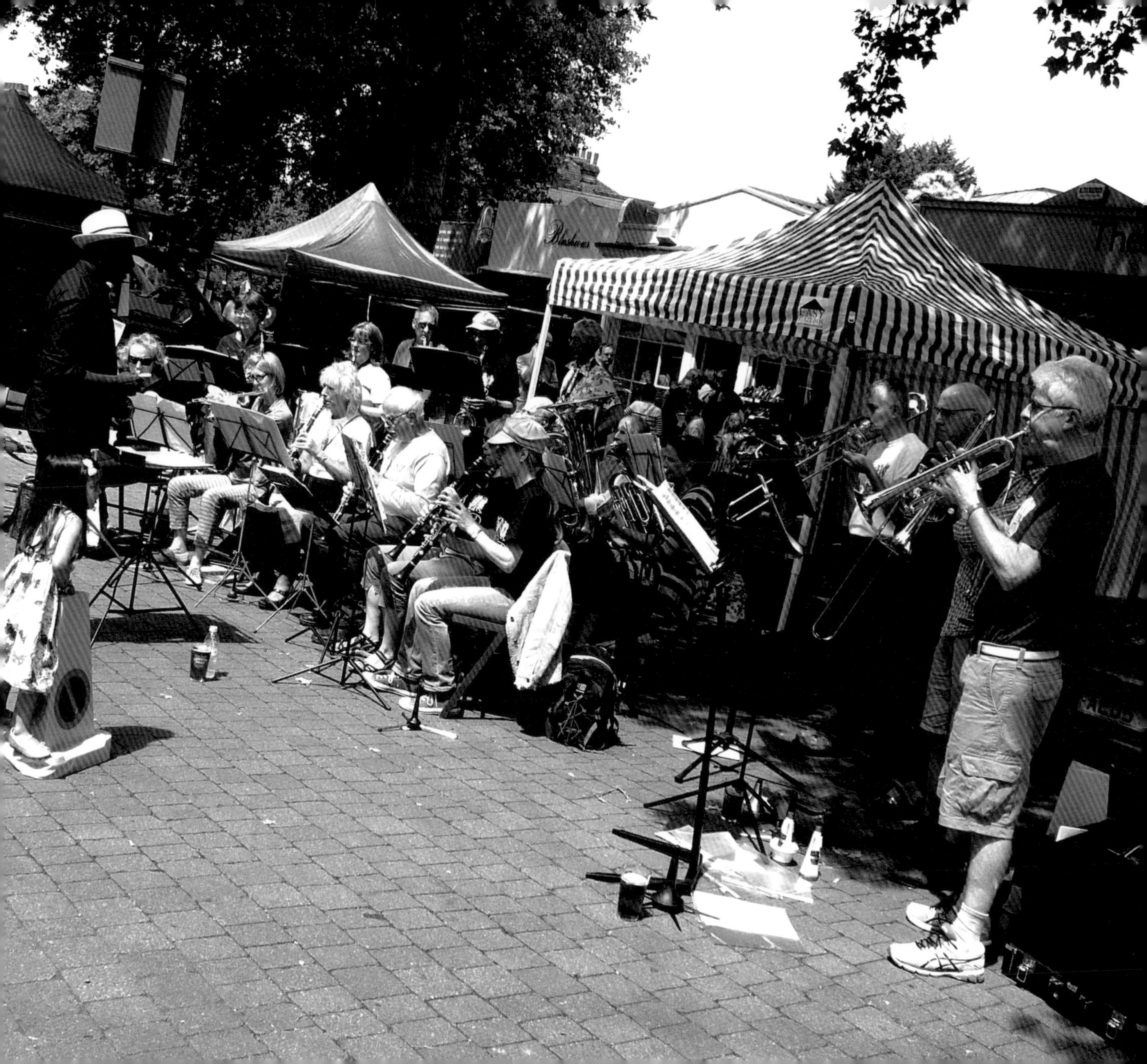

from Food On The Hill

Food on the Hill is the food store of Richmond's acclaimed A Cena restaurant and everything sold on their stall is made in the kitchens of their two shops. At Kew Village Market you'll find their traditional English raised pork pies, black pudding, sausage rolls and Scotch eggs, and also French charcuterie classics such as coarse-cut meaty pâté de campagne, and silky-smooth chicken-liver pâté, as well as jars of pesto, tomato and basil sauce, and other condiments. All perfect choices for no-bother meals. By the way, their pies won a silver and two bronze awards at the prestigious British Pie Awards at Melton Mowbray — now that is a recommendation! Paul Hughes is the chef at Food On The Hill. His two recipes here are favourites on the stall and at the shop.

Chicken liver pâté

Ideally served with some hot rustic toast and a glass of what you fancy. And be sure to eat the butter on the top — delicious!

Serves 8

650g chicken livers
1 large Spanish onion, peeled and chopped
6 peeled cloves of garlic
1 tbs fresh thyme leaves
Half a bunch of parsley, roughly chopped
650g unsalted butter, chopped into dice
2 shots of brandy
Salt and pepper

Preheat the oven to 200C/fan 180/gas 6.

While the oven is getting up to temperature, line a roasting tin with baking paper. Place the livers in it with the chopped onion, garlic and finely chopped thyme. Pop into the oven till the livers are completely cooked. This should only take about 5–7 minutes.

Place the livers into a food processor and add the chopped parsley. Pulse the livers, adding 400g of the butter little by little until you have a smooth pâté. Add the brandy and seasoning to taste. Pour into a suitable mould or individual ramekins and refrigerate.

When the pâté is set, melt the remaining butter in a small pan and allow it to separate. Discard the whey and use the clarified butter to pour a thin layer on the top. This acts as a seal. Refrigerate again. It is ready to serve when set. This pâté will keep well for a few days in a fridge, and you can also freeze it.

Terrine de campagne

You may be able to source the ingredients for this terrine from your local butcher. If not, make a pilgrimage to Paul's butchery at Food On The Hill where they are always available.

Will provide at least 10 thick slices

1kg diced shoulder of pork

250g pig's liver

500g pork fat

Large handful of fresh marjoram, chopped fine

Large handful of thyme, chopped fine

1 head of garlic, peeled and chopped fine

Salt, pepper and nutmeg to taste

200g pig's caul

Preheat the oven to 190C/ fan 170/gas 5.

Mince the pork and liver together with either a hand mincer or a food processor. Set the mixture aside in a bowl large enough to mix all the ingredients. Put the pork fat into a pan and bring it to the boil. This will soften it. Tip the fat into a food processor and purée it. Let it cool a little, then add it to the mix. Add the chopped herbs, mix well, then add the garlic and mix well again. Finally add salt and pepper as needed plus a good pinch of nutmeg.

Place the mix into an oblong terrine or into a large loaf tin lined with baking paper. Smooth the top. Divide the caul into three and use these to cover the top of the pâté. Tuck the edges around the mix inside the terrine or tin. Cover the top, first with baking paper, then with foil. Place the pâté in a roasting tin. Fill the tin with water, so that the water level is halfway up the tin and cook in the oven for 1½ hours. Cool completely and refrigerate until needed.

This pâté will keep for 7 days in the fridge. Alternatively you can freeze it but allow several hours for it to defrost. When the pâté is started, the cut end will oxidise, so it is better to cut this off each time you want to eat it.

> **REAL ALE LTD RECOMMENDS**
> **Wild Beer Co. Scarlet Fever, 4.8%.**
> A hoppy, ruby real ale which delivers flavours of bready caramel followed by citrus.

from Love By Cake

Love By Cake's stall is small enchantment. Hand-finished tiny cakes, tarts and éclairs, all beautifully iced and decorated, sparkle like little jewels. Inspired by those miniature marvels, I have chosen two recipes which can be cooked at home, giving amounts which could make larger éclairs and tarts, as we amateur cooks might find that easier than creating doll-sized dainties.

However, if you're already cooking for friends and/or family and you want to round off the meal with a delicious and exquisite mouthful or two, do visit the Love By Cake stall.

Lemon tarts

Tiny tarts — just one mouthful; medium tarts — two mouthfuls; or a tart of eight slices? Your choice. Piquant lemony filling and crisp tart shell — just add a dollop of crème fraîche. Perfection!

Makes around 30 tiny, 20 medium or 1 big tart serving 8

For the pastry

110g plain flour
Pinch of salt
50g butter
50g icing sugar
1 egg yolk
1 tbs water

For the filling

225g unsalted butter
110g caster sugar
4 eggs, lightly beaten
2 lemons, juice and grated rind

Preheat the oven to 180C/fan 160/gas 4.

Sift the flour and combine it with the salt, butter and icing sugar in a food processor and process until the mixture resembles coarse breadcrumbs. Add the egg yolk and water while the machine is on and process until the mixture forms a ball. Do not over-process – stop the machine as soon as the ball is formed. Place the pastry in a polythene bag and rest it in the fridge while you make the filling.

In a saucepan melt together the butter and sugar, take it off the heat and stir in the lightly beaten eggs a little at a time. Then stir in the lemon juice and rind. Alternatively put the melted sugar and butter mixture in a food processor, allow it to cool a little and add the eggs, lemon juice and rind, processing well between each egg.

Roll out the pastry and use it to line well-buttered or oiled 4cm or 7cm tart tins or one 25cm large tin. Prick the bases with a fork. Let the pastry rest again in the fridge for 20 minutes. Pour the filling into the tin/s and place them in the oven on a baking sheet. This will ensure the base is firm and the lemon filling sets well. Bake for 30–40 minutes. Smaller tarts will need less time, probably 15 minutes will do them. The top(s) should be a golden brown. Remove from the oven and let the tarts cool to room temperature before taking them out of the tins.

Choclate éclairs or profiteroles

Love By Cake make exquisite tiny éclairs but if you have not got the equipment or are not confident with a piping bag, profiteroles are the perfect solution.

Makes at least 20 profiteroles

For the éclairs/profiteroles
125g unsalted butter
300ml water
300g plain flour, sifted at least once
3 eggs
Pinch of salt

For the pastry cream
250ml full-cream milk
Vanilla essence
50g caster sugar
3 egg yolks
25g plain flour
Pinch of salt
25g unsalted butter

For the chocolate Icing
40g unsalted butter
25g cocoa, sifted
2 tbs milk
110g icing sugar

Preheat the oven to 180C/fan 160/gas 4.

This is an occasion when it is best to have all the ingredients weighed out before you begin.

Dice the butter and put it and the water in a medium-sized saucepan, preferably non-stick. Melt the butter and bring the mixture up to the boil. Remove it from the heat and tip all the sifted flour into the saucepan. Then beat the mixture with a wooden spoon until it comes away from the pan and forms a dough. Cool it until it is lukewarm, then beat in the eggs one at a time. Beat well after each addition. If you have a food processor you can put the dough into the bowl. Wait for it to cool, turn on the processor and add the eggs one at a time, processing well after each addition. Either way, after the eggs are beaten in, you should have a sticky dough which will hold its shape.

Line a baking sheet with non-stick baking paper. If you are going to make éclairs you need to have a piping bag and a metal nozzle approximately 4cm in diameter. Fill the bag with the choux pastry dough and pipe 7cm lengths for éclairs. Alternatively, you can make chocolate profiteroles, which taste just as delicious! Use two teaspoons to drop balls of the choux about the size of a walnut onto the lined baking sheet. Leave enough space between for them to puff to twice their size. Bake for 20–30 minutes – the éclairs/profiteroles should be a golden brown. Slice them part-way across. This lets the steam out and gives you an opening to use to fill with pastry cream. Cool them on a wire rack.

Meanwhile make the pastry cream. Add a few drops of vanilla essence to the milk and bring it up to the boil. Remove from heat. Beat the sugar and egg yolks together in a bowl until they are pale and thick. Sift in the flour and mix gently with the sugar and yolks. Then slowly add the hot milk, beating all the time. When all are mixed smoothly, clean the milk saucepan, return the mixture to the saucepan and put it back on the heat. Gently heat the mixture, beating continuously. The mixture will thicken and you should have a smooth delicious custard. Let it cool and then use a teaspoon to fill the éclairs or profiteroles.

Now make the icing. Melt the butter in a small pan. Stir in the cocoa and cook very gently for one minute. Remove the pan from the heat and stir in the icing sugar and the milk. Beat with a wooden spoon until the mixture thickens to a spreading consistency. Be patient – this can take 10 minutes. Carefully dip each profiterole in the chocolate so that approximately 50% is covered and rest them for a couple of hours so that the icing is set. For éclairs the icing must be piped. Then wait for the compliments!

A lot of work, but so worthwhile. You can freeze the profiteroles: open-freeze them on a tray, then store them in tubs – they defreeze very fast. Also, the pastry cream is excellent as a trifle topping and the chocolate icing is perfect for a chocolate cake.

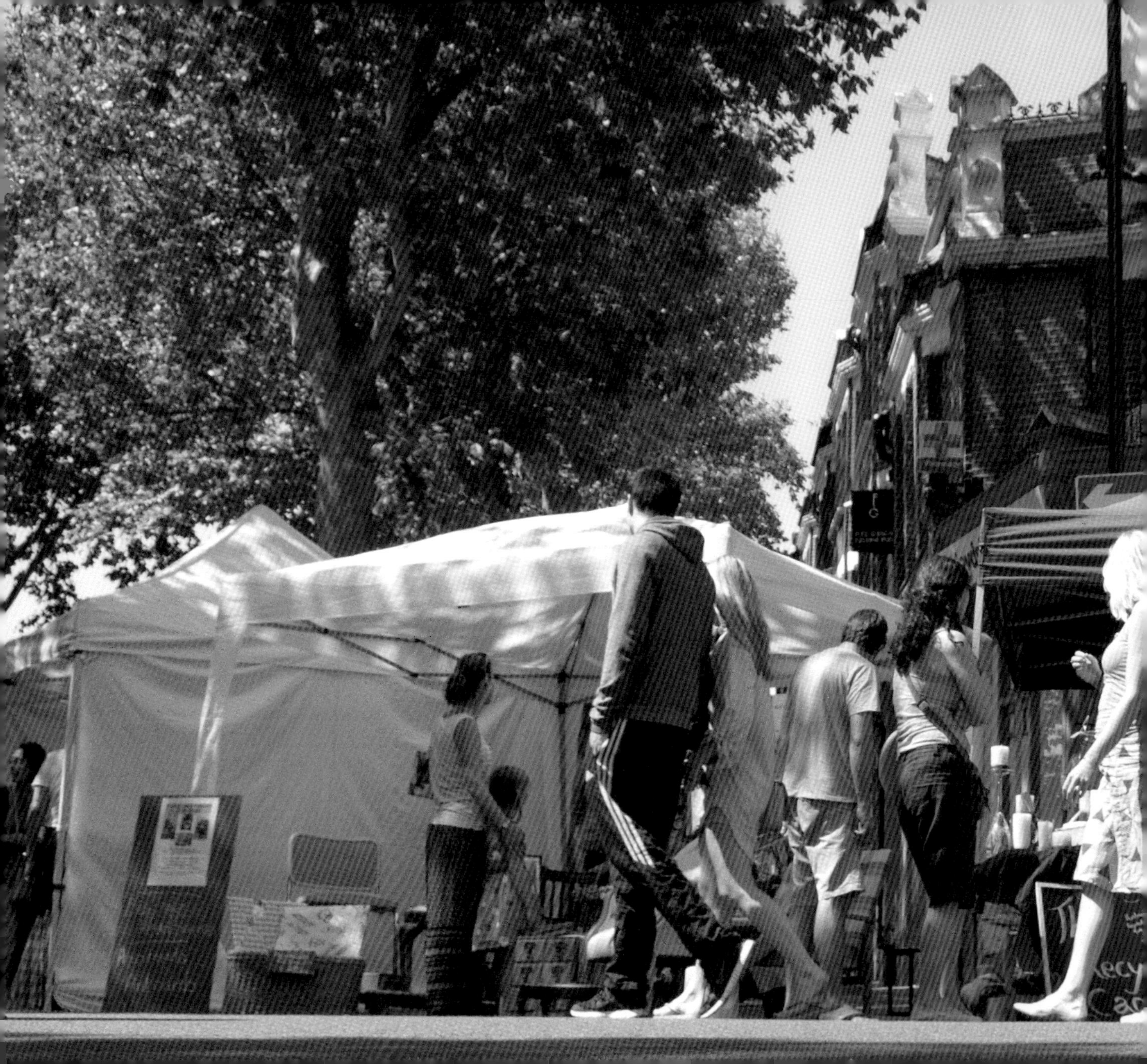

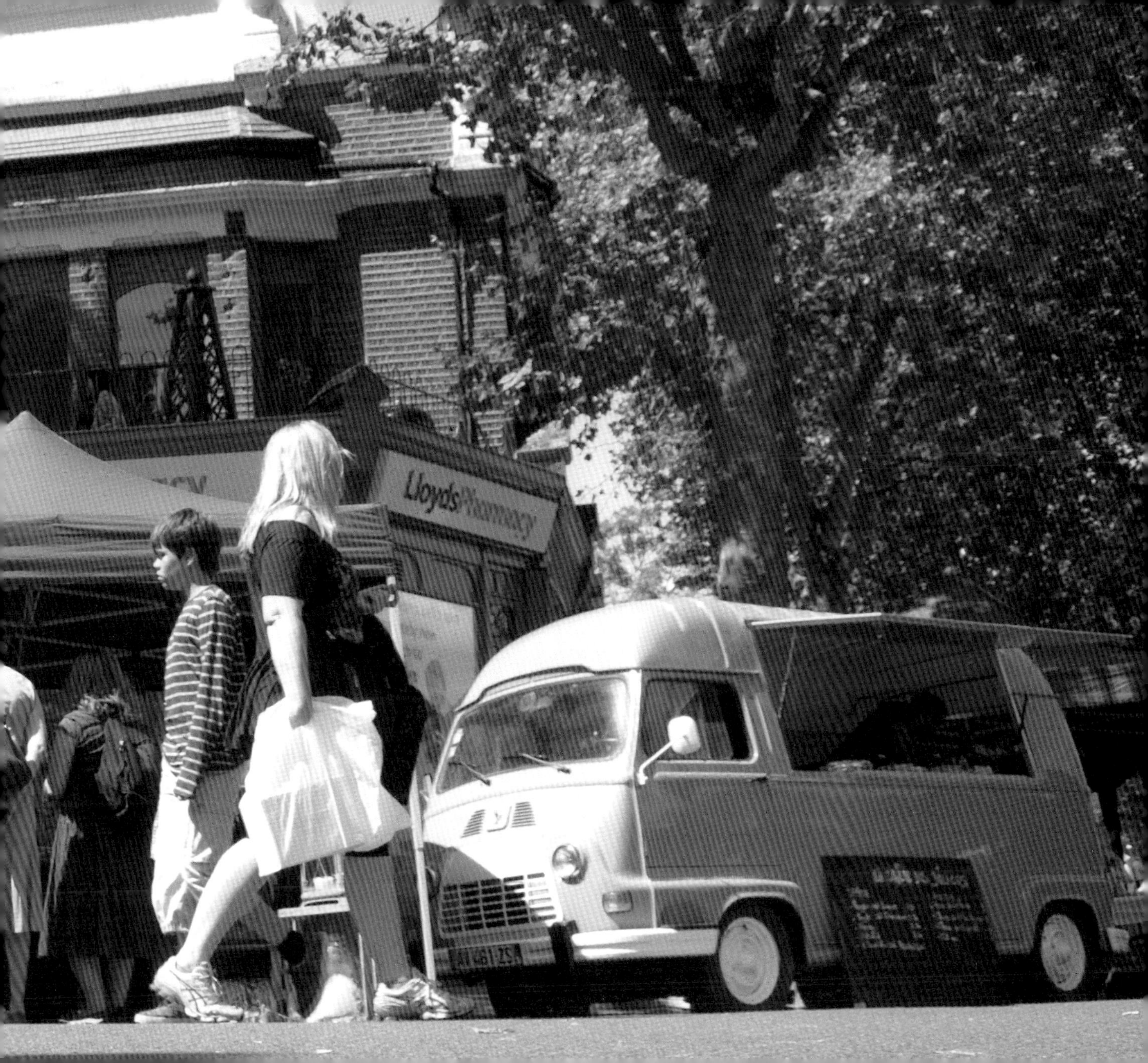
LloydsPharmacy

from Lusobrazil

Rute Diniz is Portuguese, her husband Secundo is Brazilian and she hand-bakes cakes, savouries, biscuits and breads from the traditional cuisines of both countries. When she was nine, her mother started selling breads and cakes to help fund the family and Rute's job, with her brothers, was to deliver to her customers. Now she's the baker.

Here are recipes for three of Rute's very popular specialities. The Chorizo Breads are a Portuguese recipe, the Cheese Puff Breads are traditionally Brazilian and the Pineapple Upside-Down Cake is baked in Portugal and Brazil – so it is truly Lusobrazil!

Chorizo breads

Rute's grandfather was a fisherman and he used to take these piquant rolls with him on fishing tips on the sea. They make good snacks and they're perfect for picnics and as a savoury accompaniment to soups.

Makes around 15

For the yeast mix
200ml warm water
1 tsp salt
1 tsp sugar
1 tbs dried yeast
1 tsp strong white bread flour

For the rolls
1 kg strong white bread flour
200ml warm water
1 tbs extra virgin olive oil
1 cooking chorizo ring, cut into small round slices

NB You need to begin this recipe the day before you intend to make the breads.

Place all the ingredients for the yeast mix – warm water, salt, sugar, yeast and teaspoonful of flour – in a bowl large enough to allow for the mixture to expand. Leave the mixture overnight. The next day you will find that the yeast mix has grown. Skim the foam off the top of the mix.

Preheat the oven to 225C/ fan 205C/gas 7.
Sieve the flour on to a board. Make a well in the middle and add the water, olive oil and the yeast mix. Mix well until the flour starts to form a non-sticky, elastic dough. You might have to add a little more flour. Flour a clean surface and knead the dough for 10 minutes. Put the dough back in the bowl. Cover the bowl with cling film and leave it in a warm place for an hour to rise.

Turn the risen dough out on a clean floured surface and cut it into balls. Each ball should weigh around 80g. Flatten each ball with a rolling pin. Put 4 or 5 slices of chorizo on each piece. Roll them up so the sausage is inside the dough. Make three thin cuts on the top of each bread. Lay them on a tray and bake for 15 minutes. The tops should be golden and the breads should not stick to the tray. Cool on a wire rack and serve warm or cold.

Lusobrazil pineapple upside-down cake

Moist, exotic and bitter-sweet at the same time... When I saw this luscious cake on Rute's stall and tasted a morsel, I knew the recipe must go in the book.

1 pineapple
200g caster sugar
4 free-range eggs
65ml sunflower oil
125ml water
200g plain flour
25g fine polenta flour
2 tsp baking powder
½ tsp cinnamon
½ tsp vanilla

Pereheat the oven to 180C/ fan 160/gas 4.

First peel the pineapple and cut half of it into slices. Grease a 20cm solid-bottomed cake tin.

Next make the caramel. Put 100g of the caster sugar in a small saucepan and just cover it with a little water. Heat over a moderate heat. Do not stir the caramel. After between 10 or 15 minutes the sugar will become a golden-brown syrup. Pour the caramel into the cake tin and line the base with pineapple slices. Do this as quickly as possible before the caramel sets.

Crack the eggs into a large bowl and whisk them with the rest of the sugar until they are pale and creamy. Whisk in the sunflower oil and water. Sieve the flours with the baking powder and cinnamon and gently fold them into the mixture. Lastly chop the other half of the pineapple into small chunks and fold them into the mixture with the vanilla. The more gently you do this the more the cake will rise.

Pour the mixture into the cake tin, place it on a metal baking sheet and bake for approximately 30–40 minutes. The cake is ready when a metal skewer comes out clean.

Turn it out on to a plate immediately, before the caramel sets. The pineapple and caramel topping ensures that the cake will be deliciously moist.

Brazilian cheese puff breads

Known as Pão de Queijo, these delectable puffs are found in every Brazilian home and Rute says these are 'Brazilian best of the best!' Oliver's stocks tapioca starch which is gluten- and wheat-free.

Makes around 15
400ml milk
200ml sunflower oil
2 tsp salt
500g tapioca sour starch
100g tapioca sweet starch
3 eggs
400g mozzarella cheese, diced

Preheat the oven to 180C/ fan 160/gas 4.

Put the milk, oil and salt in a saucepan and bring the mixture to just below boiling point. Sieve the sour and sweet starch into a bowl, add the hot milk and oil and blend, using an electric beater. When all is mixed together, whisk in the eggs one by one. Finally tip in the mozzarella and whisk all together until it is smooth. The consistency should be almost like a bread dough. If it seems too liquid, add a little bit more sweet starch.

Oil and water your hands and fashion balls about the size of a golf ball. Put them on a baking tray not too close together – they will puff up when you bake them. Bake them for about 15 minutes until they are light golden colour. Cool on a wire tray and serve hot or warm.

from Madame Macaroon

No marks for guessing what Jenni Davies sells on her stall, but there's also a mouth-watering spread of biscuits, cookies, biscotti and meringues.

There's always an exciting regular range of macaroons but check out her seasonal specials too – look out for blackberry, beetroot and even pumpkin macaroons. From her kitchen in south-west London Jenni bakes fresh every day using locally sourced ingredients (visit www.madamemacaroon.net to find out more).

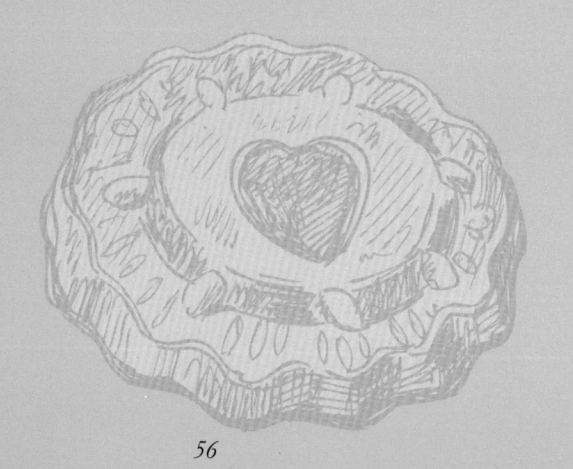

Macaroons

Here Jenni shares her recipe and method for making perfect macaroons. NB – you need a sugar thermometer to make this recipe.

Makes 40

200g caster sugar
200g icing sugar
200g ground almonds
10g cocoa powder (optional)
160ml egg whites (you can buy cartons of egg white in good supermarkets)
Extra cocoa for dusting (optional)

Preheat the oven to 150C/fan 130C/gas 2.

First prepare the macaroon biscuits. Place the caster sugar in a saucepan with 75ml cold water and stir over a high heat until the sugar is dissolved. Bring to the boil without stirring and continue boiling until the sugar syrup reaches 118C (but see below). Brush the insides of the pan with water as needed to prevent crystals forming.

Sieve the icing sugar and ground almonds (and cocoa powder if using) together in a large bowl to form the *tant pour tant*. Add 80ml of the egg whites; do not mix.

Place the remaining 80ml of egg whites in the bowl of a stand mixer and when the sugar syrup reaches 115C start whisking them on a moderate speed. When the egg whites have formed soft peaks and the sugar syrup reaches 118C pour the sugar syrup onto the egg whites in a steady stream, continuing to whisk them whilst a meringue forms. Whisk for 2 minutes then allow the meringue to cool.

Fold the meringue into the *tant pour tant* until a smooth mix is formed, similar in consistency to a cake batter. The mixture should flow smoothly (not drop) from the spoon. Once you reach this consistency, do not mix further or you will lose the air that you whipped into the meringue.

Place the mixture into a piping bag with a 1cm plain nozzle, and pipe 80 rounds about 2.5cm in diameter onto baking trays lined with non-stick baking paper. Gently tap the tray onto a bench 5 times to remove any air bubbles. Allow to dry (approximately 1 hour). The macaroons are ready to be cooked when they are touch-dry, not tacky. If you like, you can lightly dust the uncooked biscuits with sieved cocoa powder at this stage.

Once a skin has formed on the macaroons, bake them for 10 minutes. Quickly open the oven door to release any steam, and cook for a further 2-4 minutes until the macaroon biscuits are firm but not browned. Remove trays from the oven and slide the baking paper onto a dry surface to allow the macaroons to cool. Once cool, remove from paper and store the macaroon biscuits in an airtight container in the fridge until required.

Pipe your desired filling onto half of the macaroons and top with the remaining half of the biscuits, pressing gently together. Refrigerate for at least two hours.

The macaroons will last up to 7 days stored in an airtight container in the fridge or can be frozen for up to a month. Bring the macaroons up to room temperature before serving.

FILLING 1

125ml double cream

165g dark chocolate (55-70% cocoa solids), finely chopped or grated

40g unsalted butter, chopped

FILLING 2

2 tsp good-quality instant coffee

1 tbs hot water

250g unsalted butter, softened

140g icing sugar

40g ground almonds

Chocolate ganache filling
Place the cream in a small saucepan and bring to just boiling. Remove from heat and pour over the finely chopped chocolate and butter. Stir until combined and the ganache becomes glossy. Allow to cool to room temperature. The ganache should be a piping consistency; however, if it's still quite loose refrigerate it to the desired texture. Place into a piping bag with a 1cm plain nozzle.

Coffee buttercream filling
Dissolve the coffee in the hot water. Mix the butter, icing sugar and almonds together and slowly add the coffee until thoroughly combined. Place into a piping bag with a 1cm rosette nozzle.

Anzacs

These iconic biscuits were originally made to send to the Australian New Zealand Army Corps at Gallipoli in 1915 during World War One, hence ANZACS. They must have been a treat to soldiers a long way from home and on army rations.

Makes around 20

100g rolled or breakfast oats

100g desiccated coconut

50g plain flour

200g caster sugar

150g unsalted butter

1 tbs golden syrup

1 tsp bicarbonate of soda

2 tbs boiling water

Preheat the oven to 150C/ fan 130/gas 2.

Combine the oats, coconut, flour and sugar in a bowl large enough to hold all the ingredients. Melt the butter in a medium saucepan on a medium heat and add the syrup. Put the bicarbonate of soda in a small bowl and pour the boiling water over it. It will immediately start frothing up. Pour the frothy mixture into the butter and syrup in the saucepan and the mixture will double its size again. Make a well in the centre of the dry ingredients and pour in the frothy mixture. Stir well to combine everything.

When it is cool enough to handle, dampen your hands (this will stop the mixture sticking to your fingers) and take small balls from the mixture and roll each into a golf ball shape. Place on a baking sheet lined with baking paper and press each ball down. Allow plenty of space for the biscuits to spread. Bake approximately 15 minutes when the Anzacs should be golden brown. Cool on the tray.

The biscuits will keep well in an airtight tin for approximately 2 weeks.

Gluten- & dairy-free florentines

Glistening, nutty, sticky, fruity treats!

Makes around 20

125g flaked almonds

30g dried cranberries or raisins or sultanas

60ml runny honey

1 orange

Preheat the oven to 160C/ fan 140/gas 3.

Combine all the ingredients together in a bowl except the orange. Either peel the orange thinly, put the peel in the oven for just a minute, allow it to cool, cut it into slivers and add to the mixture; or take the grated rind from the orange and add as before. Stir gently until all the nuts, fruit and orange slivers are coated in honey. Place heaped teaspoons of the mixture on a baking tray lined with baking paper, allowing room for them to spread. Bake for approximately 15 minutes until deep golden brown.

Take the florentines from the oven. The honey will have spread out. Using a knife or fork, carefully push any stray nuts or berries back into a mound so that they will stick together when cool. Allow them to cool on the tray before peeling carefully from the baking parchment.

Once cool transfer the biscuits to an airtight container. Separate the biscuits from each other with non-stick paper. Eat within the next 2–3 days.

MILK BREADS

from Noggin Farm

Will and Sarah Grant were among the stallholders for our very first market in October 2011, selling the superb pork from their heritage Lop pigs. The British Lop is the rarest of the rare breeds. It's slow growing – which gives it excellent flavour – and much leaner than other heritage breeds, which means that you can have the best of both worlds.

At the market Will and Sarah have done a cracking trade in roasts, chops and ribs, and of course the sausage and bacon butties whose sizzling supplied the irresistible smell of market Sundays. However, as this book goes to press we're very sad to hear that Sarah is suffering from kidney failure, so they have had to cease trading for the present while she waits on dialysis for a transplant. Sarah and Will are much missed and all their friends and customers hope they'll be back at the market before too long.

Sweet & sour sticky spare ribs

Favourites with all ages who like to get stuck in – and sticky with it!

Serves 6-8

2 packs of 10 ribs of pork (allow about 3 ribs per person)

For the marinade

1 large onion, peeled and chopped
2 tbs peeled and grated fresh ginger
2 tbs clear honey
2 tbs brown sugar
2 tbs tomato purée
6 tbs soy sauce
100ml cider vinegar
300ml water
3 cloves of garlic, peeled and pressed

Preheat the oven to 180C/fan 160/gas 4.

Mix the marinade ingredients together in a large bowl. Cut the ribs into single bones. If they are very long chop the rib in half. Add the ribs to the marinade and leave them in it for at least a couple of hours.

Lay the ribs in a single layer in a large roasting tin lined with baking paper. Pour the marinade over the ribs, cover the tin with foil and bake for 45 minutes. Then take the foil off and continue cooking until the meat is very tender, which should take approximately 30 minutes. Alternatively, if you are barbecuing, you can do the uncovered roasting on the barbecue.

Serve them warm, not hot (you are going to eat the ribs with your fingers).

Stuffed tenderloin of Lop pork

Pork tenderloin can be dry so an apple and blue cheese stuffing makes perfect sense. Here the fresh herbs used are thyme and marjoram, but you can vary them according to what is to hand. How many does it feed? Depends on appetite! Two hungry people, possibly three – and any left over is delicious cold.

Serves 2–3
- 2 thick slices of bread
- 1 tbs onion, finely chopped
- 1 tbs chopped fresh herbs – thyme, marjoram, sage, and/or parsley are all good
- 1 apple, peeled and grated
- 50g diced blue cheese
- Salt and pepper
- 1 egg
- 1 tenderloin of pork

Preheat the oven to 180C/ fan 160/gas 4.

Put the bread in a processor and blitz into breadcrumbs. Mix the breadcrumbs with the onion, herbs, apple and cheese and season well. Bind the mix together with the egg to form the stuffing.

Using kitchen scissors, carefully cut a slit along the tenderloin (being careful not to cut right through) and open it out. Place the meat in between clingfilm and whack it with a rolling pin, so you have a piece of meat about 1cm thick. Spread the meat with the stuffing. Roll it up carefully, tie it with string to keep it together and roast it (join side up) on a roasting tray lined with a piece of foil or baking paper for 30 minutes. Take off the string and carve the pork into thick slices.

> **THE GOOD WINE SHOP RECOMMENDS**
> **Viognier Vin de Pays Les Vignes d'a Cote, Yves Cuilleron.**
> Apricot, peach and floral notes on the nose, a creamy concentrated palate with a discreet lick of oak – this white wine is a model of richness and restraint.

Pork tenderloin carbonara

Here's Noggin Farm's adaptation of the classic Tagliatelli alla Carbonara – ribbons of pasta tossed with slivers of pork in a creamy sauce speckled with chopped parsley.

Serves 4
- 400g pork tenderloin
- 1 tbs oil
- 1 medium onion, peeled and sliced
- 2 cloves of garlic, peeled and chopped
- 4 slices of bacon, chopped
- 300ml crème fraîche
- Salt and pepper to taste
- 400g tagliatelli
- 2 tbs chopped parsley
- Freshly grated Parmesan cheese

> **THE GOOD WINE SHOP RECOMMENDS**
> **Amedeo Custoza DOC 2012, Cavalchina, Italy.**
> An excellent blend of Cortese and Garganega (the grapes for Gavi and Soave respectively), this deftly balanced red wine has a velvety texture with plenty of crisp citrus and stone fruit. Partial ageing in oak casks adds breadth and richness as well.

First check the tenderloin and remove any sinews and/or membrane. This is important because you want the meat to be very tender. Slice it into thin slivers of meat suitable for stir-frying.

Heat the oil in a non-stick saucepan or frying pan large enough to contain all the ingredients and fry the onions and the garlic until they are beginning to soften. Add the bacon and the slivers of tenderloin and continuing frying until all the ingredients are lightly browned. Then slowly add the crème fraîche, stirring as you do, to make a sauce. Season with salt and pepper, turn off the heat and let the sauce rest while you cook the tagliatelli according to the packet instructions (usually about 10 minutes).

Drain the pasta, retaining the water. Reheat the sauce, adding a little pasta water if necessary and toss the pasta gently in the sauce. Add the parsley, toss the pasta again and serve immediately with a bowl of grated Parmesan so everyone can add it to their own taste.

Sausage & chorizo cassoulet

Cassoulet originated in south-west France, and spicy sausage has always been one of the signature ingredients, along with beans. Here the chorizo provides the spicy element but the traditional duck or goose is replaced with fresh sausages. This version is more affordable than the traditional dish and still tastes good.

Serves 4

| 1 tbs sunflower or olive oil |
| 1 large onion, peeled and chopped |
| 2 garlic cloves, peeled and chopped |
| 8 fat sausages |
| 2 tsp sugar |
| 1 bay leaf |
| 1 sprig of thyme |
| 100g chorizo, thickly sliced |
| 400g tin of chopped tomatoes |
| 400g tin of butterbeans or cannellini beans, drained and rinsed |
| Salt and pepper |

Heat the oil in a cast-iron casserole or saucepan that will take all the ingredients. Sauté the onion and garlic with the sausages and the sugar until the sausages are a nice golden brown. Then add the herbs, chorizo, drained beans and the chopped tomatoes.

Cover the casserole or pan, bring to the boil and immediately reduce the temperature. Add salt and pepper to taste and simmer the dish gently on the top of the stove for about 30 minutes. Serve with crusty bread to soak up the piquant sauce.

> **REAL ALE LTD RECOMMENDS**
> **Left Hand Black Jack, 6.8%.**
> Espresso and dark chocolate notes combine with herbaceous hop flavours to deliver an English-style porter.

Roast pork belly with chestnut & anchovy stuffing

This is a spectacular pork dish with dark beer for an intense flavour, inspired by one of my favourite Clarissa Dickson Wright recipes.

Serves 4-6

| 50g canned anchovies in oil |
| 3 tbs olive oil, plus extra for rubbing |
| 1 onion, peeled and chopped |
| 1 large garlic clove |
| 200g cooked chestnuts, peeled and roughly chopped |
| Salt and pepper |
| 150ml dark beer or stout |
| 1.5kg pork belly |

Preheat the oven to 230C/fan 210/gas 8.

> **REAL ALE LTD RECOMMENDS**
> **Saison Dupont, 6.5%,**
> a light, pale, spicy ale with hints of citrus, white pepper and clove.

Place a roasting tin over a medium heat and add the oil from the can of anchovies and the olive oil. Add the onion and garlic and fry for 2–3 minutes, or until softened but not coloured. Roughly chop the anchovies and add them to the pan, along with the chopped chestnuts. Season with freshly ground black pepper and pour in the beer.

Score the pork belly skin with a sharp knife at 1cm intervals and rub with salt and olive oil. Place the pork into the roasting pan, making sure it covers the chestnut mixture.

Roast for 30 minutes, then reduce the oven temperature to *160C/fan 140/gas 3* and roast for a further three hours, or until the pork is very tender and the skin is crisp and golden-brown.

To serve, thickly slice the pork belly and spoon over the chestnut mixture from the pan.

Stuffed shoulder of pork with walnut, capers & lemon stuffing

Here the pork is partnered with a zingy stuffing of walnuts, capers and lemon, inspired by a celebration dish by Clarissa Dickson Wright.

Serves 8-10

- 4 slices of white bread, crusts removed
- Olive oil
- 1 onion, finely chopped
- 75g walnuts, chopped
- 2 tsp small capers
- 1 lemon, juice and grated rind
- 5 fresh sage leaves
- Salt and freshly ground black pepper
- 1 large free-range egg
- 2kg boned pork shoulder
- 250ml vegetable stock
- 1 tbs lemon juice

Preheat the oven to 230C/fan 210/gas 8.

For the stuffing, cut the bread into small cubes and pulse in a food processor until they form breadcrumbs. Heat 3 tbs olive oil in a large frying pan over a medium heat and gently fry the onion until soft and translucent. Add the breadcrumbs and fry for a further 2–3 minutes, then remove from the heat. Stir in the chopped walnuts, capers, lemon juice and rind and chopped sage leaves and season to taste with salt and freshly ground black pepper. Set aside to cool for 10 minutes, then break the egg into the pan and mix thoroughly to combine with all the stuffing ingredients.

Lay the pork shoulder skin-side up and score the meat at 2cm intervals with a sharp knife. Rub all over with salt and olive oil. Turn the meat over and spread the stuffing over the meat. Roll the meat up and tie securely with kitchen string.

Place into a roasting tray and roast for 25 minutes. Then turn the heat down to *160C/fan 140C/gas 3* and roast for a further 1 hour 30 minutes or until the juices run clear when the pork is pierced at its thickest part. Remove the pork from the oven, cover with aluminium foil and set aside to rest for 10 minutes. Pour away the fat, keeping the meat juices, add the stock and lemon juice, test for seasoning and bring to the boil. Thickly slice the pork shoulder and serve with mashed potato and the gravy.

THE GOOD WINE SHOP RECOMMENDS
Barbera d'Alba, Vigna Pozzo Renato Corino, one of the best Barberas around. A red wine, it has the classic balance of dark cherry and bramble fruit and fresh acidity that will complement this dish perfectly.

REAL ALE LTD RECOMMENDS
Sambrook's Junction, 5%.
This is brewed as a traditional English bitter, using only English hop varieties, lots of crystal malt and a touch of roasted barley, which give it an inviting auburn colour and a spicy, rich and malty taste.

Pork in cider with a suet pie crust

Pies and suet pastry are both English food traditions. Here they are combined to produce a hot pork pie that is robust and filling.

Serves 4

- 1 tbs oil
- 1 large onion, peeled and sliced
- 2 thick slices of unsmoked back bacon, diced
- 500g diced casserole pork
- 2 tsp wholegrain mustard
- 300ml sweet cider
- 300ml vegetable stock
- Pepper and salt to taste

For the pastry

- 250g self-raising flour
- 110g suet
- Salt and pepper
- 1 egg yolk

Preheat the oven to 180C/fan 160/gas 4.

Heat the oil in a frying pan or saucepan and soften, then brown the onions. Add the bacon and fry it until the dice are beginning to brown. Add the pork and brown the meat. You will need to keep shaking and scraping the pan to stop the meat from sticking. Stir the mustard into the cider and stock and pour the liquids over the meat. Bring everything up to the boil, then immediately turn the heat down. Cover the pan and simmer the meat very gently for one hour.

Take out the meat, bacon and onion and use it to fill a pie dish. Tip the sauce over the meat. If there is too much liquid, boil it fast without a lid until the sauce has reduced sufficiently to just cover the meat. Check for salt and pepper and set the pie aside while you make the pastry.

Sieve the flour into a bowl and add the suet, and a litttle salt and pepper. Then, spoon by spoon, add water to make a manageable, softish dough. Roll it out on a well-floured surface to cover the pie. Wet the edges of the pie dish to make the pastry stick, and if you have any dough left over you can cut it into leaves to decorate the pastry lid. Cut a couple of holes to let the steam out, brush the top with egg yolk and bake for approximately 30 minutes or until the pastry is golden.

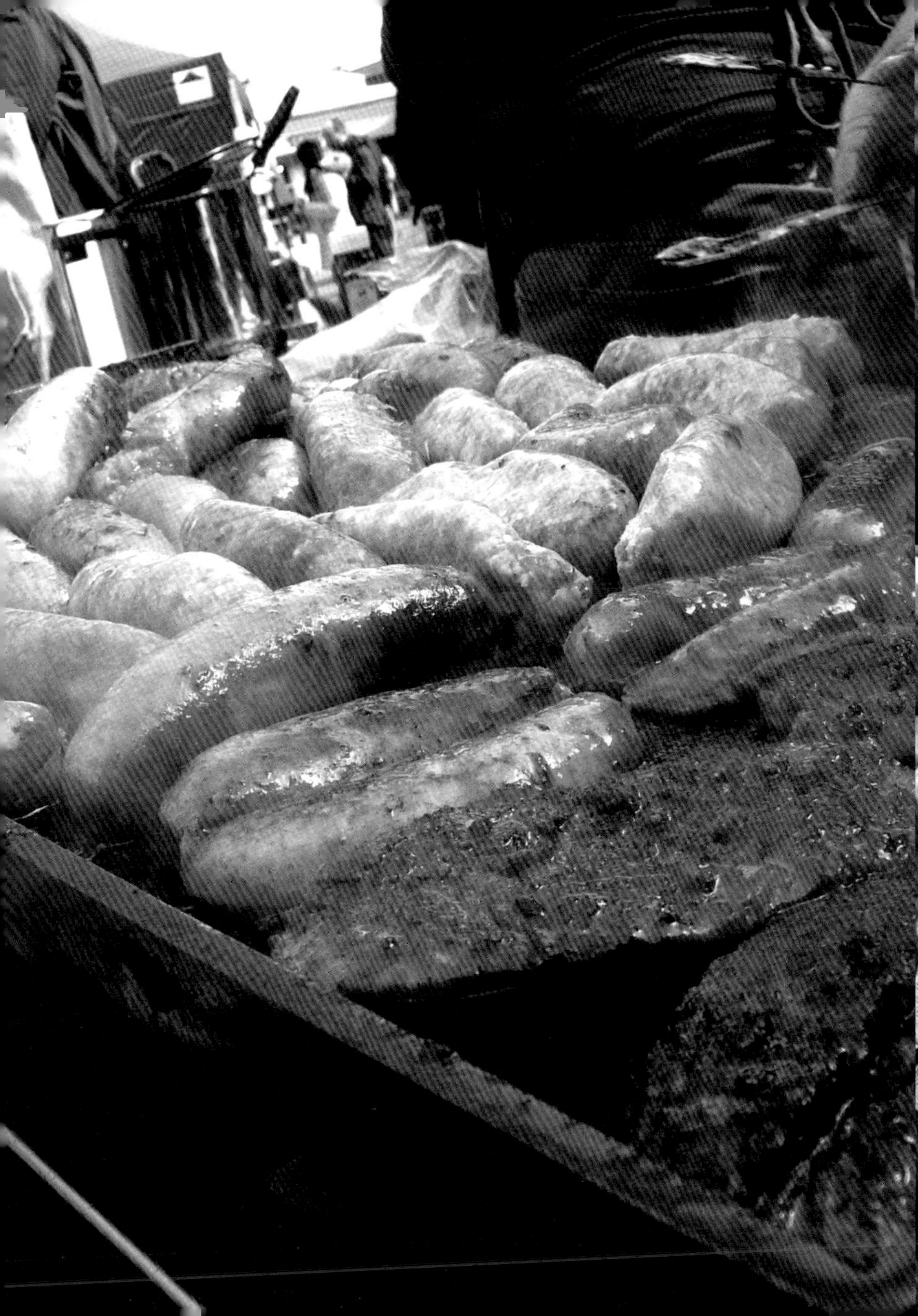
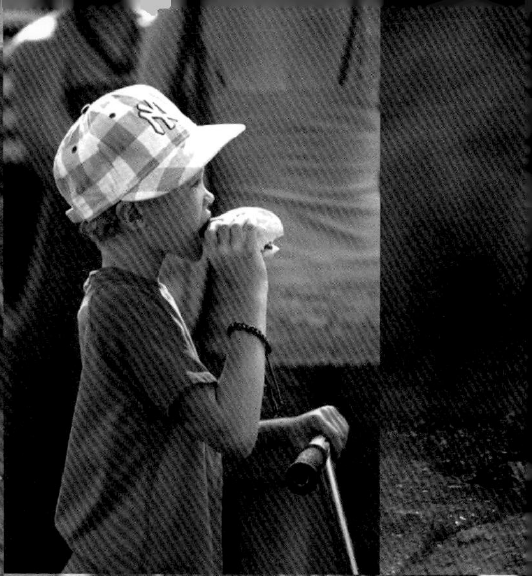
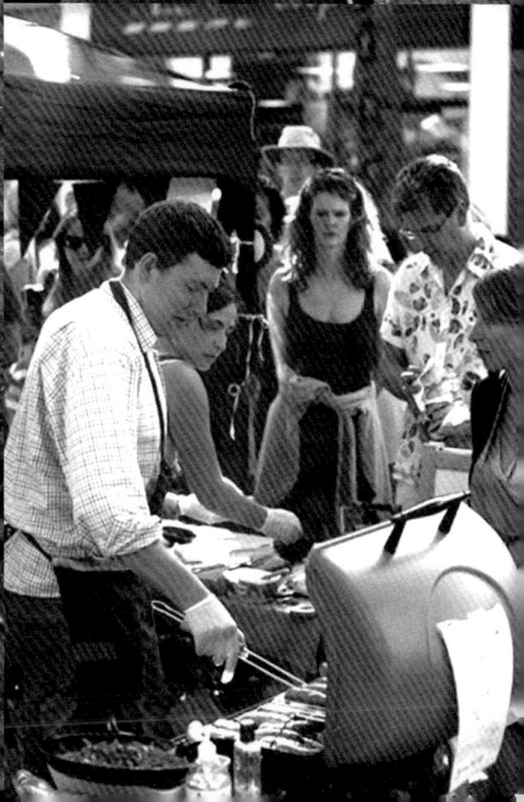

from Norbiton Cheese Co

Norbiton Cheese began small. Now it has access to over 600 cheeses from the UK and abroad and a client base that includes top-class restaurants, delicatessens and caterers. Standards are high. 'We only sell farmhouse and small quantity artisanal cheese,' says Gabriel Marton. On the stall you may find familiar favourites, but these are the best of their kind, all award winners and many Supreme Champions at British Food and World Cheese Awards. There's also a selection of all kinds of less well-known names — at the market, let Gabriel guide you through the different varieties to make your own choice.

May I also direct you to his website — www.norbitoncheese.co.uk? It is wonderful, with fascinating facts about cheese and over 20 recipes using different varieties. The recipes here are from that list. Oh, and it has a Cheese Wedding Cake which you can order for any special occasion — what a brilliant idea!

Risotto with four cheeses

This is a rich creamy risotto. The flavours will vary a fraction every time you make it, as do the Italian cheeses.

Serves 4

- 50g unsalted butter
- 1 tbs olive oil
- 8 shallots, peeled and chopped fine
- 1 clove of garlic, crushed
- 300g risotto rice such as Vialone Nano, Carnaroli or Arborio
- 125ml white wine
- 900g vegetable stock
- 50g Gorgonzola cheese, cut into cubes
- 50g Fontina cheese, cut into cubes
- 50g Taleggio cheese, rind removed and cheese cut in cubes
- 100g Parmesan cheese, freshly grated
- Salt and pepper to taste
- A handful of flat-leaved parsley, coarsely chopped

Heat the butter and olive in a frying pan, wok or heavy-based saucepan over medium heat. Add the shallots and cook for about five minutes until they are soft but not browned. Add the garlic and mix well. Add the rice and stir until the grains are well coated and glistening. Then pour in the wine and stir until it has been completely absorbed.

Keep the pan on a medium heat and add the stock, a ladleful at a time. Allow the stock to simmer until it has been absorbed by the rice. Keep stirring all the time as you add the stock. Reserve one last ladle of stock. After 20 minutes or so, the rice should be tender but still have a bite to it.

Then add all the chopped Gorgonzola, Fontina and Taleggio cheeses, 50g of the Parmesan, parsley, and the last ladle of stock. Give it one last stir to mix in the cheeses. Check for salt and pepper, cover the pan and let the risotto rest for a couple of minutes.

Spoon into bowls, sprinkle with the rest of the Parmesan and serve. A green salad and bread complete the pleasure.

> **THE GOOD WINE SHOP RECOMMENDS**
> **Blason Cabernet Franc, Isonzo, Friuli Doc, Italy.**
> A fresh, lively, fruity red from northern Italy, this will cut the richness of the cheeses.

Beetroot soup with Beenleigh Blue cheese croûtons

Beautiful to look at – and just as good to taste. The cheese tempers the sweetness of the beetroot beautifully.

Serves 4

50g butter
2 onions, peeled and chopped
225g uncooked beetroot, peeled and chopped
1 large potato, peeled and chopped
800ml vegetable stock
A thin baguette of bread
100g Beenleigh Blue cheese

REAL ALE LTD RECOMMENDS
Hacker Pschorr Hefe Weisse, 5.5%.
A dark golden colour with a white, thick head, this has aromas of sugar, some hints of bubble gum and spices with notes of citrus. The upfront sweetness is well balanced with a nice bitterness.

Heat the butter and gently sauté the onions until soft. Add the beetroot and potato, stir once and add the stock. Bring the soup back to boiling, cover and simmer for approximately half an hour. By this time the potato and beetroot should be cooked through. Let the soup rest a couple of minutes, then purée with a hand liquidiser or a food processor until it is smooth, return it to the saucepan and bring it back to just below boiling.

While the soup is cooking, heat the grill and cut the baguette into thin round slices. Mash the cheese and spread it thickly on the bread slices then pop them under the grill until the cheese is just beginning to melt.

Ladle the soup into large soup plates or bowls and top each helping with the Beenleigh Blue croûtons.

Cheddar cheese & Calvados fondue

Serve this with a long baguette cut into chunks to dip into the fondue.

Serves 4

1 clove of garlic, peeled
185ml dry cider or white wine
2 tbs Calvados or other apple brandy
400g mild Cheddar cheese, coarsely grated
1 tsp cornflour
Salt and pepper and freshly grated nutmeg

REAL ALE LTD RECOMMENDS
Rocky Head Pale Ale, 6.5%.
An intensely flavoured pale ale with pine cone and citrus notes from the American and New Zealand hops.

Rub the fondue pot or heavy saucepan with the garlic clove and set it on the heat. Pour in the cider or wine and the Calvados. Heat until the liquid starts to bubble. Then add the cheese and stir until the mixture begins to bubble. Add the cornflour and stir again until the mixture is just up to the boil. Keep the fondue on the heat. Season to taste with nutmeg, black pepper and salt if you need it. Remember, cheese is salty already so be careful.

The fondue is now ready. Divide the bread so that people can dip their own chunks into the fondue. Keep it bubbling slowly and when you have reached the bottom of the pan you should find a delicious crispy crust which you can scrape off and savour.

Endive salad with Roquefort, celery & walnuts

Here it's not just taste that's important. The textures of the crunch of the celery and walnuts together with the crumbly cheese complement the flavour.

Serves 4

- 4 heads of endive, sliced
- 2 celery stalks, thinly sliced
- 75g Roquefort cheese, crumbled
- 50g walnut pieces
- A handful of flat-leaf parsley, finely chopped

For the dressing

- 1 tbs wine vinegar
- 1 tsp Dijon mustard
- 4 tbs extra virgin olive oil
- Salt and pepper to taste.

First make the dressing in the bowl in which you are going to serve the salad. Put the vinegar in the bowl, add the mustard and whisk with a fork until they are well blended. Then whisk in the oil, a spoon at a time, until you have an emulsion. Check for salt and pepper.

Just before you want to serve the salad, add the endive, celery, Roquefort and walnuts. Toss gently and serve with a basket of sliced French bread.

> **REAL ALE LTD RECOMMENDS**
> **Rochefort Trappistes 10, 11.3%.**
> A rich, dark, malty ale with hints of plum, raisins, spice and mocha.

Caramelised shallots with Fourme d'Ambert on puff pastry

You can serve this tart hot, cold or warm. Gabriel's preference is warm – it's easier to cut, you don't burn your mouth and the textures and tastes are perfect.

Serves 4-6

- 250g fresh or frozen puff pastry
- Small amount of egg white
- 100g unsalted butter
- 500g small shallots, peeled and cut in half
- 1 tsp sugar
- 125ml double cream
- 115ml yoghurt
- 250g Fourme d'Ambert or Oxford Blue cheese
- 1 tbs fresh thyme leaves (optional)
- Salt and pepper to taste.

Preheat the oven to 180C/ fan 160/gas 4.

Roll out the pastry in a 20cm circle and score about 2.5cm from the edge with a fork. This will help the edge to rise when cooking. Place the pastry on a lightly oiled baking sheet and let it rest in a cool place while you make the onion filling.

Melt the butter in a frying pan with the sugar, add the shallots and cook gently until they become soft and golden brown. Tip the shallots and butter into a bowl and set aside to cool to room temperature.

Mash the cheese with the cream and the yoghurt and add the thyme and salt and pepper to taste. Spread the mixture over the pastry, leaving 2.5cm gap round the edge. Place the shallots over the top. You can use any left-over egg white to brush the edges, to give a shiny finish. Bake on the middle shelf of the oven for approximate 30 minutes.

> **REAL ALE LTD RECOMMENDS**
> **Odell 90 Shilling, 5.3%.**
> Richer than most amber ales, this is smooth and deeply satisfying, with a crisp, clean taste. The name comes from the old Scottish method of naming a brewery's beer, based on original gravity and resulting tax rating.

Cornish Yarg
Made at Lynher Dairies, Cornwall
Delicious semi-hard cheese is creamy under the rind and slightly crumbly in the core. Young, fresh, tangy taste and is made by hand in open round vats.
Cows, pasteurised. Veg
£22.00/Kg

Wild Garlic Yarg
Made at Lynher Dairies, Cornwall
More recent development to nettle covered Yarg. Creamy and crumbly, the leaves impart a delicate garlic flavour quite unlike any other garlic cheese you may have tried.
Cows, pasteurised. Veg
£22.00/Kg

Gubbeen
Made by Tom and Giana Ferguson, near Schull, Co Cork, Ireland
Named after the bay where the cows graze, this is a medium washed rind with a fresh milky taste and mild buttery flavour.
Cows, pasteurised
£26.00/Kg

Blue Monday
Made by Alex James and cheese guru Juliet Harbutt at Carnedale.
Alex James may find some fame after his time with the Britpop band Blur, but he deserves New Order too. Really Blur, isn't it, but very Mad Blue.
Cows, pasteurised, veg
£22.00/Kg

Blue
...Grubb family, Beenkmoont,
...semi-soft, blue veined, medium blue cheese with a creamy texture. Blue is a more recent creation from the ...which produces a sister cheese Cashel ...cheese made using from cow's milk.
...s, pasteurised
£24.00/Kg

from Nut Knowle Farm

At Nut Knowle Farm in Sussex, Paul Toni makes a comprehensive – and award-winning range of vegetarian, pasteurised goat's cheeses.

Pedigree British Toggenburg and British Saarinen goats are reared on a natural diet of cereals and lush meadow hay. They are milked every day, producing a really delicately flavoured milk which is perfect for making quality cheese.

Piquant or mild, hard or soft, the cheeses are equally good to cook with or eat fresh – see the whole range at www.nutknowlefarm.com. Paul's recipes emphasise the broad spectrum of rewarding dishes that can be made with his delicious cheeses.

Beetroot, walnut & goat's cheese salad

This makes a lovely and unusual starter. Simply divide the salad onto individual serving plates and dot each portion with the goat's cheese.

Serves 4-6

- 60g walnuts
- 6 small beetroots, boiled and peeled. You can buy these vacuum-packed in most supermarkets which will save a lot of time
- 1 tbs extra virgin olive oil
- 1 tbs balsamic vinegar
- 1 pinch dried oregano or 1 tsp fresh oregano leaves
- 75g soft goat's cheese – Wealdway Mature is Paul's suggestion
- Pepper and salt to taste

Heat a dry frying pan over a medium heat and add the walnuts. Toast until lightly browned. This will take about 3–5 minutes – shake the pan and watch them closely as they burn very easily. Set aside to cool.

Dice the beetroots into 2.5cm chunks and put in a salad bowl big enough to hold all the ingredients. Add the olive oil, balsamic vinegar, oregano, and the cooled walnuts. Toss the salad gently and dot the top with half teaspoonfuls of goat's cheese.

REAL ALE LTD RECOMMENDS
Brooklyn Lager, 5.2%. This is amber-gold in colour and displays a firm malt centre supported by a refreshing bitterness and floral hop aroma. Caramel malts show in the finish.

Goat's cheese & vegetable tarts

Goat's cheese, onions and balsamic vinegar is a match made in heaven.

Makes 8 individual tarts

500g shortcrust pastry
25g butter
1 large red onion, peeled and sliced
2 tsp fresh thyme leaves (or ¼ tsp dried thyme)
2 tbs balsamic vinegar
1 egg, beaten
200g hard goat's cheese, cut into chunks
200g cherry tomatoes
70g rocket to garnish

Preheat the oven to 180C/ fan 160/gas 4.

Put the pastry on a floured surface and roll out into eight 10cm x 13cm rectangles. Put them on shallow baking sheets, either greased well or lined with baking parchment, to rest in the fridge while you are cooking the onion mixture.

Melt the butter in a pan and stir in the sliced onion, thyme leaves and balsamic vinegar. Cook gently, uncovered, for about 15 minutes. Leave it to cool.

Bake the pastry rectangles for 15 minutes. Cool on a wire rack. Then return them to the tin and brush each with beaten egg. Spread the onion mixture over each pastry, not quite to the edge. Top with the goat's cheese chunks and the halved cherry tomatoes. Bake for 15 minutes. Scatter the tarts with rocket and serve with a side salad.

> **REAL ALE LTD RECOMMENDS**
> **Hitachino Nest Pale Ale, 5.5%.**
> One of the best pale ales from Japan, though made in traditional English brewing method with English malts and hops. It has a malty, hoppy note which creates a rich, full-bodied flavour.

Chicken breasts stuffed with goat's cheese

This is incredibly easy and incredibly tasty – serve it with hot new potatoes and green vegetables. At Christmas time you could use two tablespoons of cranberries instead of the damsons.

Serves 4

4 chicken breasts, skin on
200g creamy goat's cheese
12 damsons or small plums (not too ripe)
A little oil
Pepper and salt to taste

Preheat the oven to 180C/ fan 160/gas 4.

> **REAL ALE LTD RECOMMENDS**
> **Weinstephaner Hefe Weissbier, 9.5%.**
> Aromas of peach, orange, banana, yeasty bread and clove spices all follow into an earthy and smooth wheat flavour.

Create a pocket under the skin of each chicken breast. This is best done carefully with your fingers – you don't want to make a hole in the skin nor separate the skin totally from the breast. Divide the goat's cheese into four and spread it as evenly as possible under the skin of each breast.

Stone the damsons or plums, cut them in half and use them to top the cheese. Smooth out the skin and, so far as you can, tuck the edges round the breast. Brush the skins with a little oil and season with pepper and salt. Put the breasts on a tin lined with baking parchment and roast in the oven for about 30 minutes.

Goat's cheese & rocket pasta

Here's a quick lunch or supper. Total preparation time? The time it takes to cook the pasta!

Serves 2

- 225g pasta, such as fusilli
- 150g hard goat's cheese
- 4 tbs extra virgin olive oil
- 150g cherry tomatoes, chopped in half
- 2 cloves of garlic, peeled and chopped fine
- Salt and pepper to taste
- 40g rocket leaves

> **THE GOOD WINE SHOP RECOMMENDS**
> **Pouilly Fumé Les Cocques, Domaine Patrick Coulbois, Loire, France.**
> Goat's cheese and Sauvignon Blanc is a classic marriage and this Pouilly Fumé will be a perfect complement to this dish.

Bring a large pan of water up to the boil and cook the pasta according to the packet instructions. It should take about 10 minutes. While the pasta is cooking, crumble the goat's cheese into a bowl large enough to take everything.

Add the oil, the tomatoes and garlic. When the pasta is cooked, drain it and toss it gently in the bowl with the other ingredients. Salt and pepper it to your taste. At the last minute, scatter the rocket leaves over the pasta and toss gently one more time. Serve immediately.

Pasta with goat's cheese, courgettes & lemon

Another swift and tasty lunch or supper dish.

Serves 2

- 2 large courgettes, sliced
- 1 lemon
- 3 tbs olive oil
- 1 medium onion, peeled and chopped
- 1 clove of garlic, peeled and chopped
- 200g short pasta, such as conchiglie or farfalle
- 150g soft goat's cheese
- Pepper and salt
- Parsley to garnish

> **REAL ALE LTD RECOMMENDS**
> **Westmalle Tripel, 9.5%.**
> A strong and spicy Trappiste-style beer, with lots of citrus rind and floral notes. Quite a big yeasty character greets you in the aroma and flavour.

Cut the courgette slices into strips. Cut a thick slice from the middle of the lemon and chop it as finely as you can. Heat 2 tbs of the oil in a frying pan and fry the onion, garlic and the chopped lemon until they are soft but not coloured. Set aside.

Start cooking the pasta according to the packet instructions (usually takes about 10 minutes). While the pasta is cooking, re-heat the onion mix gently and add the courgette strips. Fry very gently – you want the courgette still to have a little a little bite to it. Take the pan off the heat and stir in the goat's cheese, the last spoonful of olive oil and the juice of the lemon. Season with pepper and salt. Drain the pasta and stir in the sauce. Garnish each plateful with a little chopped parsley.

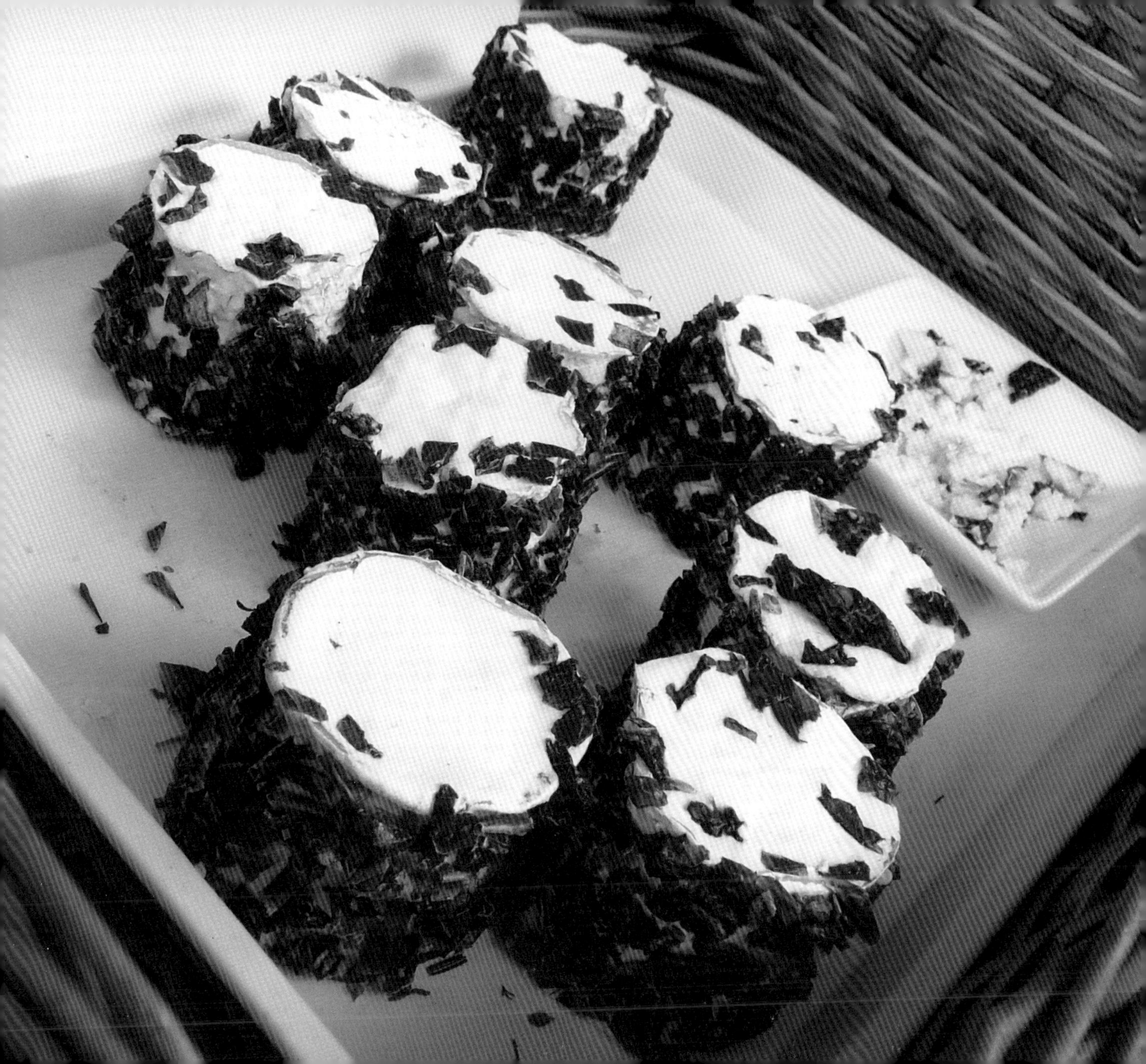

from The Nutty Lady

The Nutty Lady's stall has a different seasonal theme each month, but the nuts are a year-round favourite: hand-made, spicy caramelised nuts made to her own recipe in her Kew kitchen. The mix contains almonds, pecans and walnuts (but never any peanuts, which aren't really nuts at all but a type of pea). Log onto www.nuttyladyltd.co.uk to find out more.

If you can stop the family raiding the larder and eating them first, these tasty nuts go well with cheese Salt and add a special touch to salads. Kathy Thexton, aka the Nutty Lady, has given us two delicious salad recipes. In each case the crunch of the nuts and their spicy sweet flavour are the perfect complement to the other ingredients.

Nutty Lady coleslaw

Here's a crunchy, flavourful, sweet-and-sour salad dish.

Serves 8

For the dressing
- 2 tbs yellow mustard seeds
- 150ml cider vinegar
- 2 tbs golden caster sugar

For the salad
- Half a white cabbage, shredded
- Half a green cabbage, shredded
- 1 small red onion, peeled and thinly sliced
- 3 large carrots, peeled and grated
- 265g caramelised spicy nuts

First make the dressing. Toast the mustard seeds in a dry pan on the hob until they pop.

Add the vinegar and sugar and stir until dissolved. Take off the heat.

Combine the vegetables and toss them in the hot dressing. Sprinkle the nuts over the coleslaw before serving.

Nutty Lady quinoa, feta & squash salad

Quinoa is a delicious, nutty alternative to rice. It originates from Peru and Colombia, where it has been a staple for thousands of years.

Serves 4 as a side dish

- 1 small butternut squash (approx 450g), peeled and cut roughly into 3cm chunks
- 50ml olive oil
- 250ml vegetable stock
- 125g quinoa
- Salt and pepper
- 75g caramelised spicy nuts
- 100g feta, crumbled roughly
- 4 tbs chopped parsley

Preheat the oven to 200C/ fan 180/gas 6.

Toss the butternut squash with the olive oil and roast for 35 min. Keep an eye on it and add a little more oil if it seems to be getting too dry.

Bring the stock to the boil, add the quinoa and season with salt and pepper. Bring the pan back to boil, then reduce the heat to low, cover with a lid and simmer for 12 min or until all liquid has been absorbed.

Cool a little then place in large bowl with butternut squash, nuts, feta and parsley. Gently toss the salad to combine all the ingredients and serve.

from Oliver's Wholefood Store

Again, not one of our stalls, but such a Kew landmark and source of superb ingredients that Oliver's simply had to have a place in this book!

Founded by Sara Nokavik in 1989, Oliver's Wholefood Store was one of the first shops to specialise in organic food and has grown impressively from its modest beginnings. It is now four times larger, a wonderful, award-winning emporium of all things organic.

Here you can find organic pasta, organic beer, organic cheese and organic nuts. The vegetable display is as gorgeous to look at as it is good to taste.

There are also herbal remedies and supplements, and on most weekdays a nutritionist is in the shop to advise customers. Sara's mission 'to raise awareness on how food is made' has succeeded brilliantly.

Split green pea & mint soup

Sara says: 'This soup is cheap, easy to make and nutritious. We have served it on market Sundays and everybody loved it.'

Serves 3–4

1.5 litres of vegetable or ham stock

1 medium onion, peeled and chopped

1 clove of garlic, peeled and chopped

300g split peas

1 tbs fresh chopped mint (or 1 tsp dried mint or 2 tsp concentrated mint sauce)

Salt and pepper to taste

Juice and grated rind of 1 lemon (optional)

Fresh mint to serve (optional)

Put all the ingredients except the lemon in a saucepan and bring it to the boil. Then cover it and reduce the heat immediately. Simmer the soup for approximately 30 minutes. Test and try the peas – they should be soft. Add salt and pepper to taste and blitz in a food processor or with a hand-held blender.

Add the lemon juice and rind, if using, and serve piping hot with a little fresh mint in each soup bowl, if possible. Crusty bread is the perfect accompaniment.

Irish stew

This recipe comes from Northern Ireland and is perfectly partnered by the Red Cabbage Pickle. Buy the vegetables from the wonderful display of organic produce at Oliver's, which is where you'll also find the pot barley, and the lamb from the Stilemans' stall at the market.

Serves 3–4

1 tbs vegetable oil

450g neck fillet of lamb, cut into chunks

1 large onion, peeled and sliced

2 medium carrots, peeled and cut into short lengths

1 celery stick, chopped

450g new potatoes, scrubbed

150g pot barley

Approximately 1 litre of vegetable stock

Salt and pepper to taste

Heat the oil in a cast-iron casserole and fry the meat and onion together until nicely browned. Take the casserole off the heat and add the carrots, celery, potatoes and pot barley. Stir and add the vegetable stock to cover the meat and vegetables.

Bring the casserole back to the boil and then either simmer very slowly on the top of the stove or stew gently in the oven *(preheated to 150C/fan 130C/Gas 2)* until the meat is tender and the vegetables are cooked but still have a little crunch (it should take around an hour and 15 minutes). Season to taste and serve with red cabbage pickle.

> **THE GOOD WINE SHOP RECOMMENDS**
> **Chateau Fourcas Dupre, Listrac en Medoc.**
> Ruby in colour, this claret is balanced and harmonious with elegant, silky tannins after nearly a decade of bottle age. Dark fruits vie with coffee and toast flavours on the palate while the finish is lengthy and satisfying.

Red cabbage pickle

This is a Northumbrian recipe. You need to start it at least four days before you want to serve it but it's well worth the wait!

Makes 6 jars (350g each)

1kg red cabbage

1 large onion, peeled

2 tsp salt

1 tbs soft brown sugar

600ml cider or wine vinegar

150g caster sugar

½ tsp black peppercorns

½ tsp cloves

2 cinnamon sticks

Slice the cabbage and onion finely and mix with salt in a large bowl. Put all the rest of the ingredients in a saucepan and bring to the boil, stirring while the sugar dissolves. Transfer the liquid to a china or plastic bowl and leave both mixtures overnight.

Next day, put the cabbage and onion into jars, packing them as tightly as you can. Pour over the vinegar mixture, being sure to fill the jars right up to the top. Screw on the lids and leave the pickle at least three days before using. The pickle will last months and even improve in flavour.

Pot barley & puy lentil salad

Rich in fibre and proteins, nutty, healthy, tasty and lovely to look at – what's not to like?

Serves 4 as a main dish or 6 as a side dish

- 4 small sweet potatoes
- 100g cherry tomatoes
- Olive oil
- 100g pot barley
- 100g puy lentils
- 1 lemon
- One small head of broccoli, cut into florets
- Salt and pepper to taste
- Coriander leaves to garnish

For the dressing

- 1 tbs wholegrain mustard
- 1 tbs cider vinegar
- ½ tsp cumin seeds
- 3 tbs extra virgin olive oil

Preheat the oven to 180C/fan 160/gas 4.

> **THE GOOD WINE SHOP RECOMMENDS**
> **Lois Gruner Veltliner, Kamptal, Austria.**
> Light and crisp green fruit flavours with a hint of spice are backed up with a racy, zesty minerality. This white wine is great on its own but will also do justice to this hearty salad.

Line a large baking tray with baking parchment. Scrub the sweet potatoes and slice them fairly thinly. Lay the potato slices on one half of the tray, the tomatoes on the other. Drizzle a little oil on them and roast until the potato slices are soft in the middle. Set aside to cool.

While they are cooling, place the pot barley in a saucepan with 350ml of water and boil for 15–20 minutes. The barley should be soft but still a little bit nutty. In a separate saucepan do the same with the lentils. Rinse the barley and lentils in cold water, drain and put them in a salad bowl large enough for all the ingredients. Add 1 tbs of olive oil with the juice and grated rind of the lemon, and stir.

Steam or boil the broccoli florets for 2–3 minutes, drain and refresh them in cold water. Drain them again and add them to the barley and lentils, together with the sweet potato slices and the tomatoes.

Whisk together the mustard, vinegar, cumin seeds and the 3 tbs olive oil, then pour the dressing over the salad and toss gently so that all the ingredients are coated. Scatter the coriander leaves over the salad, which is now ready to serve.

Crunchy nut crumble

Crumble is one of those dishes you can feel guilty about eating. Not this crumble – the oats provide fibre, the nuts are nutritious and even the sugar is very special. Made from the nectar of coconut blossoms, it's unrefined, it's organic and it has the most amazing flavour and texture.

Serves 4

- 2 large or 4 medium Bramley apples
- 2 tbs water

For the topping

- 100g jumbo oats
- 100g porridge oats
- 1 tbs sesame seeds
- 50g chopped pecans or walnuts
- 100g Biona organic coconut palm sugar (use soft brown sugar if you cannot source this)
- 150g butter

Preheat the oven to 180C/fan 160/gas 4.

Peel and chop the apples and spread them evenly over an ovenproof dish. Add the water. Combine the oats, sesame seeds, chopped nuts and the sugar in a roomy bowl and mix them together. Chop the butter fine, add it to the mixture and rub it in with your hands.

Spread the mixture evenly over the apples and bake for 30 minutes. The crumble should be golden brown and crispy.

Remove from the oven, allow the crumble to cool a little and serve it warm with cream, crème fraîche or yoghurt.

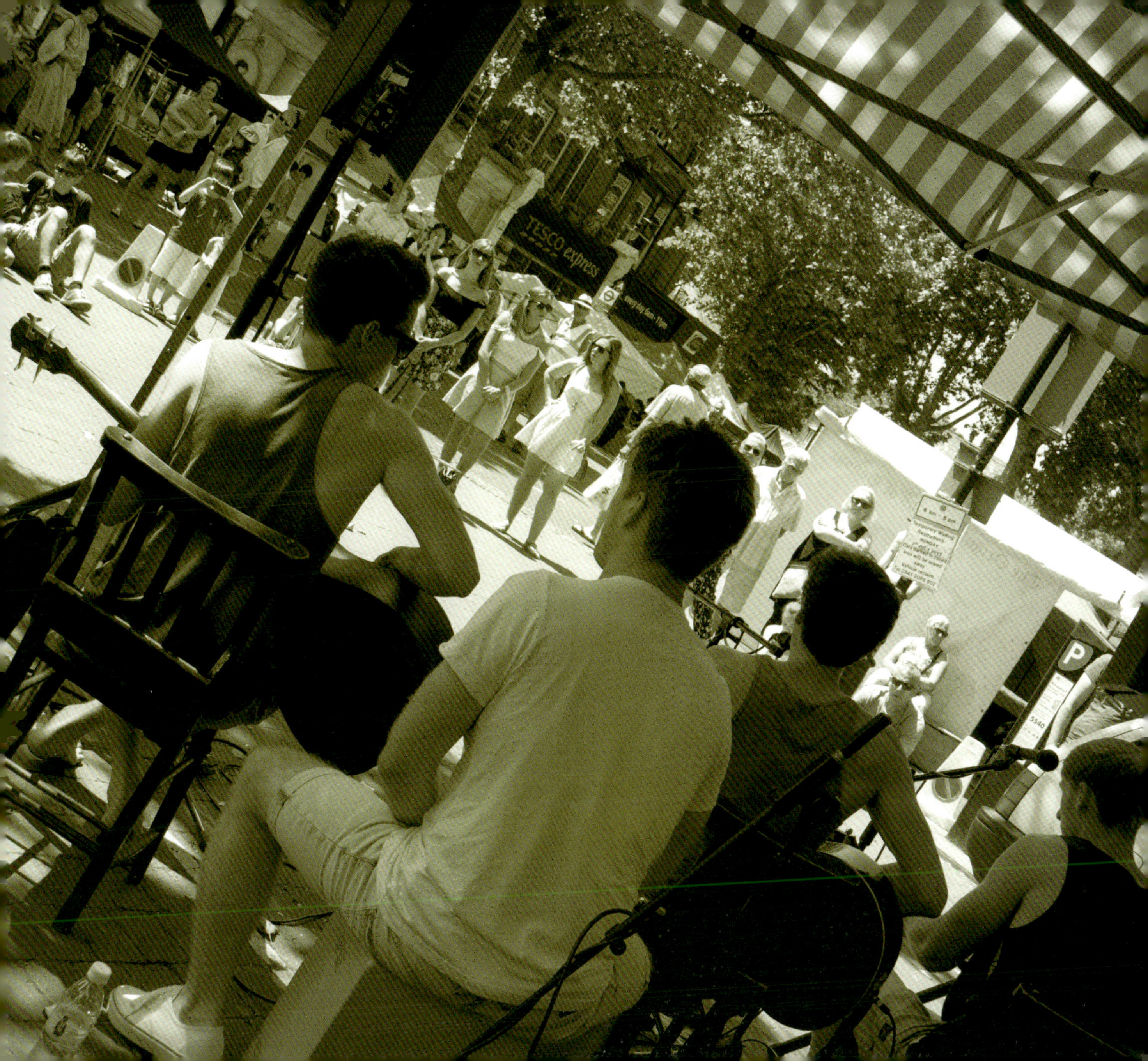
TESCO express
P

from The Portland Scallop Co

Jamie Walker is based near Chesil Beach and most of the fish he sells will have been caught on the Dorset or Devon coast. His business is of course seasonal: at different times of the year he brings bass, bream, monkfish, lemon sole, grey mullet, mackerel, plaice, scallops and prawns to the market, and most of his fish is already gutted and scaled.

Jamie's scallops are particularly sought-after and he has given us a recipe for these delicious shellfish. The other recipes are ones I've made using his fabulously fresh fish.

Baked mullet with white wine

Mullet is a fish not often seen but I've bought some beauties from Jamie's stall. This recipe is loosely based on Elizabeth David's Mulet au Vin Blanc from her Mediterranean Food, published in 1950. The aniseedy, slightly chunky fennel is a perfect contrast to the delicate flesh of the fish.

Serves 2

- Olive oil
- 1 head of fennel, finely chopped
- 1 grey mullet, cleaned and gutted
- 2 tbs chopped parsley
- 50g fresh breadcrumbs, white or brown
- 1 large onion, peeled and chopped fine
- 2 cloves of garlic, peeled and finely chopped
- 200ml white wine
- Pepper and salt

Preheat the oven to 180C/fan 160/gas 4.

THE GOOD WINE SHOP RECOMMENDS
Le Clos Jordanne, Village Reserve, Chardonnay, Niagara, Canada.
This is a rich and lusciously delicious oaked Chardonnay from Niagara – who knew the Canadians make great wine?

Heat 1 tbs olive oil and gently fry the fennel until soft. Stuff the fish with the fennel, 1 tbs parsley and half the breadcrumbs. Any fennel that is left over can join the onions, which are going to form a bed for the fish. Heat 2 tbs olive oil in a roasting tin large enough to take the fish and sauté the onions and garlic gently for about 5 minutes until they are well coated and just beginning to soften.

Place the fish on the bed of onion and garlic and season well. Brush the skin with olive oil. Add the wine and scatter the remainder of the breadcrumbs over the dish. Bake uncovered in the oven for approximately 15 minutes. Test the fish at this point: the flesh should be white and come away from the backbone. Leave it baking a little longer if you think it is not quite cooked, but keep an eye on it because it can dry out very fast. If you do not want to serve the fish immediately, turn the oven off and cover the dish with foil.

When you serve the dish, garnish the top with the remaining parsley. Steamed or boiled new potatoes are a good accompaniment.

Seafood pie

Fish Pie is the ultimate comfort food. You can vary the recipe by changing the fish – salmon or smoked mackerel, say, instead of smoked haddock. If anyone's allergic to shellfish, leave out the prawns and increase the amount of fish you use by 100g. You can even parboil the potatoes, slice them and lay them in a layer on the top of the fish and sauce to produce a gratin. It's your choice.

Serves 4

200g fresh white fish fillet (haddock, hake, cod or monkfish are suitable)

200g smoked haddock or cod fillet

800ml full-cream milk

750g potatoes, peeled

100g butter

2 tbs flour

2 tbs chopped parsley

Pepper and salt

100g peeled cooked prawns

Nutmeg

Preheat the oven to 160C/ fan 140/gas 3.

Put all the fish except the prawns in a frying pan and pour over the milk, reserving about 100ml (to be used to make the mashed potato). Cover with a lid or foil and gently simmer for 5 minutes to infuse the milk. Watch it carefully because it can boil over very easily. Meantime, chop the potatoes into chunks and boil them until soft. Drain and set aside until you need them.

When the fish is cooked drain the pan, reserving the milk to make the sauce. Melt three-quarters of the butter in a pan (non-stick if possible). When it is all melted, stir in the flour. Beat the mixture with a wooden spoon and allow it to cook gently until the flour and butter are a biscuit colour. Then pour in, a little at a time, all the fish-infused milk bar a cupful. As you do so, stir well with a wooden spoon. Keep stirring for about 3–5 minutes after all the milk is in the saucepan. If you think the sauce is too thick, add more milk. Season with salt and pepper and stir in the parsley. Take off the heat and set aside.

Put the cooked fish in an oven-proof dish. Tear the fillets apart so that you have good big chunks of fish. Add the prawns to the fish then pour over the sauce, ensuring that it covers all the fish. Set the dish aside for the sauce to cool and thicken while you mash the potatoes.

Clean out the saucepan that you have cooked the potatoes in and use it to melt the retained butter and milk. Season with salt, pepper and ground nutmeg. When the liquid is hot, take the pan off the heat, add the cooked potatoes and mash vigorously until you have a really creamy mash. Top the fish with the mash, spread it evenly and fork up the top. You may have to wait a little for the fish to cool and thicken before you put the mash on the top. This is important as the layers of fish and potato should be separate when the pie is served.

Place the pie in the preheated oven and bake for approximately 40 minutes until the top is nicely browned and the pie is beginning to bubble at the edges. Serve with a green salad.

REAL ALE LTD RECOMMENDS
St Austells Brewery Admiral's Ale, 5%. A slightly sweet strong malt with a soft hop bitterness to finish.

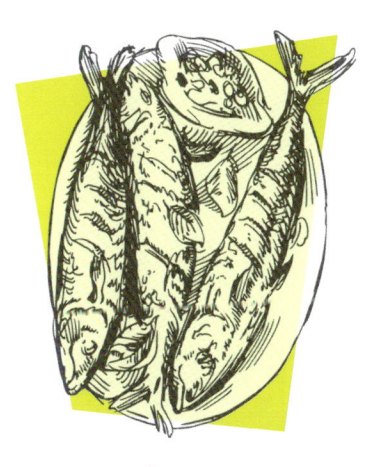

Dived scallops in the shell

Scallops deserve to be expensive: the flavour, the texture, the colour – all is fishy perfection. So a recipe for scallops should allow the true salty flavour to win through. Jamie's recipe is perfectly simple and simply perfect.

Serves 4

12 dived scallops in their shells
Cayenne pepper
25g garlic butter *
1 lemon
A fistful of parsley
Preheat the grill

REAL ALE LTD RECOMMENDS
Westmalle Tripel, 9.5%.
Strong and spicy with lots of citrus rind and floral notes. Quite a big yeasty character greets you in the aroma and flavour.

For garlic butter

1 large clove of garlic
50g salted butter

Shuck (cut) the scallops from their shells and retain the scooped side of the shell. (If you buy the scallops from Jamie, he will already have done this for you.) Place 3 scallops in each of the 4 curved shells. Sprinkle with cayenne pepper – it's spicy so be careful – and add 1 tsp garlic butter to each shell. (Fishmongers and supermarkets often have garlic butter for you to add your fish or it's simple enough to make – see below.)

Place the scallops in their shells under the grill for 2 minutes only each side. Don't be tempted to grill them for longer – they are cooked in an instant.

Remove from heat and grate the lemon rind over the fish. Squeeze the lemon and divide the juice between the shells. Scatter parsley over each shell and serve immediately with brown bread and butter to mop up the juice.

Soften the butter, crush the garlic and mix very well. Chill until needed.

Don't worry if you think you have too much for the scallops. Garlic butter will keep for at least a month in the fridge (or 3 months in the freezer) and can enhance all kinds of dishes or be used to make garlic bread.

Plaki

Plaki is served as a Greek fish meze – different versions are found all over Greece. Essentials are firm white fish steaks, tomatoes, olive oil and white wine, onions and garlic. In this recipe, leeks, pine nuts and raisins add a slightly exotic taste to the core ingredients. Each helping should have a good handful of chopped parsley added at the last minute.

Serves 4

3 tbs olive oil
1 small onion, peeled and chopped
2 large leeks, cleaned and chopped
200g tomatoes, roughly chopped
100ml white wine
25g raisins
400g monkfish, cod or haddock fillet, as thick as possible, cut into four pieces
Pepper and salt to taste
50g pine nuts
2 tbs chopped parsley

REAL ALE LTD RECOMMENDS
Camden Hells Lager, 4.6%.
This has the pale, crisp body of a Pilsner with gentle hops, soft malt, lemon and pepper.

Heat the olive oil in a frying pan large enough to hold all the ingredients. Fry the onion gently for about 5 minutes then add the leeks and tomatoes. Mix all together, fry for a further 5 minutes then add the wine and the raisins, making sure that all is well mixed. Cover the pan and simmer the vegetable mixture for 10 minutes.

Then make room in the mix for the four pieces of fish. Allow the mixture to come gently to the boil. Immediately turn the heat right down to that fish is poaching in the vegetable mix. Cover the pan and simmer for 10 minutes then turn off the heat. Don't be tempted to cook it any longer or the fish will break up. Salt and pepper to taste.

Toast the pine nuts in a dry pan until golden, scatter them over the top with the chopped parsley and serve with new potatoes or steamed rice.

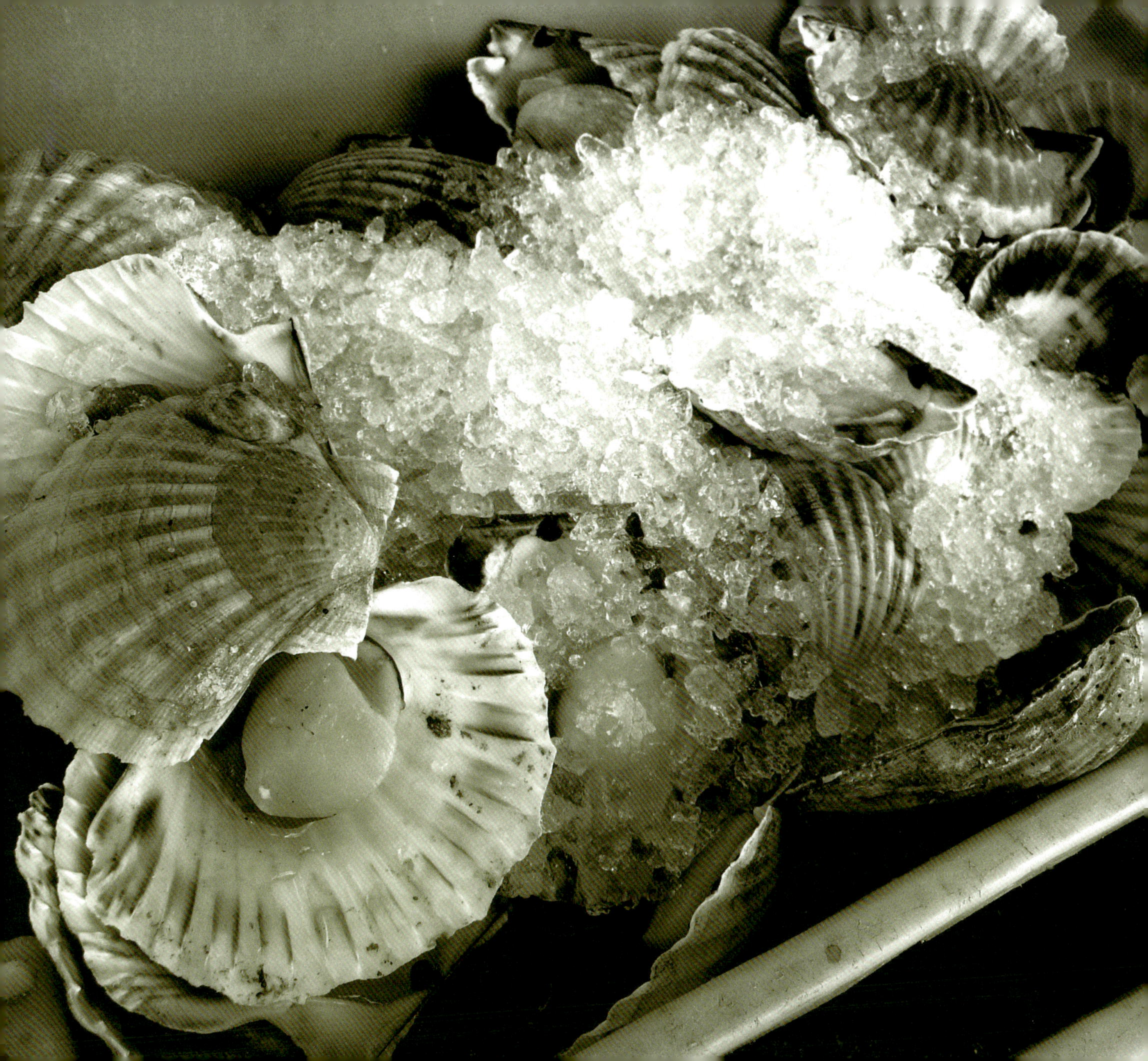

from Ruben's Bakehouse

Igor Occhiali bakes home-made artisan breads using a long fermentation process and organic flours. His stall at the market is piled high with loaves at 10am but you have to come early because they disappear quickly.

If you are too late for the bread stall, do visit his shop in Twickenham (see his website www.rubensbakehouse.com for details). At Ruben's Bakehouse (named after Igor's son) loaves are kneaded, shaped and baked before your eyes. You can buy all the breads that are on the stall and other Italian specialities. There's good Italian coffee in the café and at times great pizzas are on the menu as well.

Igor and his manager, Marco, are both from Italy (Igor from Veneto and Marco from Sardinia), where each region has its own food traditions. Of course, bread is an essential ingredient of each of their recipes here.

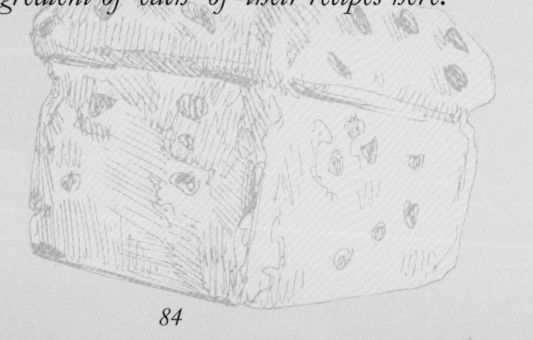

Pappa pomodoro

This is delicious as a light lunch or supper.

Serves 4

3 cloves of garlic, peeled
1 small onion, peeled
4 tbs extra-virgin olive oil
1 red pepper, chopped
400g fresh or canned tomatoes
1 tsp sugar
200g stale unsalted bread (Igor recommends Pugliese – like a denser, chewier ciabatta)
750ml vegetable or chicken stock
Salt and pepper to taste
Fresh basil to serve

Slice the garlic and the onion coarsely and sauté in 2 tbs olive oil. Add the red pepper. Chop the tomatoes and add to the garlic and onions with spoonful of sugar. Cover and cook for at least 10 minutes (fresh tomatoes might need 15 minutes) at medium-low heat, stirring regularly and adding a bit of warm water if it starts to dry up.

Cut the bread into large cubes and add to the tomatoes. Mix and keep stirring for 2–3 minutes, or until the bread is well mixed in with the tomato sauce. Add 500ml of stock and stir until the bread and tomato mix becomes a *pappa* – a mush. Check after 15 minutes and add an extra 250ml of stock if necessary. Take the lid off and keep cooking until most of the liquid has evaporated and the pappa is thick.

Divide it into four bowls, swirl the rest of the olive oil over each bowl of fragrant pappa, garnish with fresh basil leaves – and *buon appetito!*

La ribollita

This wonderful soup takes some time to make and it is traditionally left overnight for the flavours to develop. It is well worth the waiting. Igor suggests the best bread to use in this soup is Hamland Sourdough. Accompany it with more of the crusty bread and there you have it – a meal in a bowl. NB: you do need to start this recipe the day before you are serving it.

Serves 6–8

225g dried cannellini beans

For the cooking liquid:

1 small onion, peeled and chopped; 1 celery stalk, chopped; 1 sprig of rosemary; 1 sprig of thyme; 3 cloves of garlic, peeled and chopped; 750ml water.

5 tbs extra virgin olive oil
1 medium mild onion
½ tsp dried crushed chilli
Salt
2 ripe tomatoes, peeled, deseeded and chopped
1 tbs tomato paste
3 potatoes, cut into cubes
2 carrots, cut into cubes
1 small leek, chopped
3 celery stalks, chopped
300g cavola nero or Savoy cabbage, shredded
2 cloves of garlic, chopped
3 or 4 sprigs of fresh thyme
4 sage leaves
1 sprig of rosemary

Soak the beans in cold water for 12 hours or overnight, then drain and rinse.

Put the beans in a large cast-iron pot or heavy saucepan, add all the cooking liquid ingredients and simmer until the beans are well done. This will take about 1½ hours. Lift the beans out of the liquid with a slotted spoon. Keep the cooking liquid complete with vegetables and herbs. Purée three-quarters of the beans in a food processor. Stop before they become a smooth purée – you want them to be quite coarse. Strain the cooking liquid, discarding the vegetables and herbs.

Put the olive oil into the pot in which the beans were cooked. Add the onion and chilli and sprinkle with salt. Fry them gently for about five minutes, then add the tomatoes and the tomato paste and cook for 2 or 3 minutes. Next add the bean purée. Stir the mixture over the heat for a couple of minutes. Then add the potatoes, carrots, leek, celery, cavolo nero and the garlic and herbs.

Measure the bean liquid and add water to make it up to 1.5 litres. Pour it over the soup, taste and add salt if necessary. Bring the soup to the boil, reduce the heat, cover the pot and simmer over the lowest possible heat for an hour or so. Leave overnight,

The next day preheat the oven to 180C/fan 160/gas 4.

To serve

1 Spanish onion
6–8 slices of country-style bread
2 cloves of garlic, cut in half
2 tbs extra virgin olive oil

THE GOOD WINE SHOP RECOMMENDS
Poggioargentiera, Morellino di Scansano 'Bellamarsilia' Tuscany. A Sangiovese-based red wine from the deep south of Tuscany near the coast in the Maremma – Sangiovese ripens more easily here in the greater warmth of this region and typically gives luscious full-bodied reds with juicy ripe cherry and dark fruit notes. This has a more accessible style than many Chianti, with slightly softer acidity.

Mix the whole beans into the soup. Slice the onion very finely and arrange it over the surface of the soup. Put the pot into the oven and cook until the onion is tender. This will probably take about ¾ of an hour. Rub the bread with the halved garlic cloves, put it on an oven tray and bake until crisp. Keep an eye on it – it can burn.

Put the bread into individual soup bowls and ladle the soup over it. Drizzle a little olive oil over each bowl and serve with lots more of the bread to soak up the juice.

Sardinian pane frattau

This recipe is based on the traditional, unleavened Sardinian bread 'pane carasau', softened using vegetable or lamb stock and transformed into a sort of lasagna, supporting layers of tomato sauce and grated Pecorino cheese and topped with a poached egg. Marco suggests using the bread called 'carta da musica' (it's also known as 'pane frattau' and you should be able to find it in an Italian delicatessen).

Serves 4

600g ripe tomatoes, chopped
2 tbs olive oil
1 clove of garlic, peeled and cut into slivers
1 onion, peeled and coarsely cut
Salt and freshly ground black pepper
A handful of fresh basil leaves
800ml lamb or vegetable stock
8 thick slices of bread
150g freshly grated Pecorino cheese made in Sardinia, Italy. Choose a mature 'stagionato'
4 extra-large eggs

Preheat the oven to 100C/ fan 100/gas ¼.

Place four soup plates to in the oven to warm. Then make the sauce. Mix the chopped tomatoes in a medium-sized saucepan with the olive oil, garlic, onion, salt and pepper to taste and half the basil leaves; simmer for about 20 minutes. Add water if it seems to be reducing too much.

Then heat the stock to boiling point, put one slice of bread on each soup plate, pour 100ml of the hot stock over it and let it soak for 5 minutes.

Pour some tomato sauce, straight from the stove, over each slice and spread it out gently. You should use about one third of the sauce for the four plates. Scatter grated cheese over each bread slice. Again, you should use about one third of the cheese for the four plates. Keep the plates warm while you prepare the next layer, and keep the stock and tomato sauce hot on the stove.

Put the second sheet of bread in a dish, pour 100ml of the broth over it and let it soak for 5 minutes. Carefully transfer the bread onto the first plate to cover the original slice.

Repeat this three more times for the other three plates. Divide half of the remaining tomato sauce and grated cheese between the four plates. Keep the plates warm in the oven while you poach the eggs.

Half-fill a medium-sized saucepan with water and add salt to taste. Break 1 egg in the water and, using a small spoon, carefully fold the white over the egg yolk, and simmer for 4 minutes. Using a slotted spoon, transfer the poached egg onto the bread and tomato sauce of one of the dishes. Repeat the same procedure with the other 3 eggs. Add the last of the tomato sauce and sprinkle the remaining grated cheese over the plates and serve.

THE GOOD WINE SHOP RECOMMENDS
Vermentino 'Samas', Agricola Punica, Sardinia.
A blend of 80% Vermentino and 20% Chardonnay, this medium-bodied white is full of fresh apple flavours with underlying minerality and the barest hint of tropical fruit.

Zuppa gallurese

This is not actually a soup. Apparently the name may be derived from inzuppare, which means to soak in Italian. This is a rich creamy mix of cheese and bread, first soaked in stock and then baked until bubbling in the oven. In Sardinia this is served at all kinds of feasts including weddings.

Serves 4

1 litre lamb or vegetable stock

Italian bread (any sourdough loaf would be good)

1 clove of garlic

250g Pecorino cheese

250g Parmigiani cheese

A handful of chopped parsley

250g Fontina cheese

Preheat the oven to 180C/ fan 160/gas 4.

Heat the stock until boiling. Slice the bread. You need sufficient slices to allow three layers of bread in the ovenproof dish. Toast the bread and rub each slice on both sides with garlic. Grate the cheeses into three different bowls. Chop the parsley and mix it with the grated Parmigiani.

To assemble the *zuppa*, put a layer of toasts in an oven-proof dish suitable for four. Cover with a mixture of half the grated Pecorino and half the Parmigiani and parsley. Cover the cheese with another layer of toast. Cover the second layer with the rest of the Pecorino and Parmigiani. Add a final layer of toast, pour over the stock to wet all the toast, then sprinkle the grated Fontina on the top.

Bake for approximately 15 minutes, or until the cheeses are melted and the top is golden brown.

THE GOOD WINE SHOP RECOMMENDS
Montessu Agricola Punica, Igt Isola dei Nuraghi, Sardinia.
This red wine is bursting with character and fruit with intense flavours. It has notes of liquorice, dried fruits, spices and herbs with elegant, ripe tannins. There is a hint of spice in the finish.

from C & S Stileman

Chris and Sam are a mother-and-son partnership, farming near Oxted in Surrey, producing lamb and rose veal. The lambs are traditionally reared, almost entirely on grass, which means they grow and mature slower, resulting in tender meat with a good colour and an excellent flavour. The Stilemans control the breeding so they have lamb to sell all the year round. They also rear beef calves for rose veal, a welfare-friendly alternative to European veal. The meat is a delicate pink, a result of careful husbandry and the freedom for the animals to move around.

Chris is well aware of how expensive it is to feed a family today, so three of her recipes use either veal or lamb mince. However, she's also included two celebration dishes which are perfect for larger occasions; the quantities given here for both are for 6–8 but it would be easy to double or treble the amounts.

Lamb burgers with minty yoghurt dressing

Lamb, mint and peas are a classic match. Here all three combine to make very tasty burgers.

Makes 4 medium burgers

400g lamb mince
2 tbs fresh chopped mint or mint jelly
110g peas, cooked, cooled and roughly mashed
Salt and pepper to taste

Minty yoghurt dressing

4 tbs Greek yoghurt
1 tbs fresh mint
Salt and pepper

Mix all the ingredients together and add salt and pepper. Divide the mix into four parts. Wet your hands and shape the burgers. Chill them in the fridge for at least 20 minutes.

Grill, fry or barbecue them for around 3 minutes each side. Serve them with Minty Yoghurt Dressing.

Mix the yoghurt and mint together. Add salt and pepper to taste.

Casseroled lamb with apricots

Lamb with apricots was a favourite at Tudor banquets. Chris has cooked this casserole as a celebration dish for a wedding but it's equally good as a no-fuss Sunday lunch.

Serves 6–8

3 tbs olive oil

2 medium onions, peeled and sliced

½ tsp cayenne pepper

½ tsp paprika

1kg casserole lamb, cut into 2cm dice

800g chopped tomatoes (fresh or tinned)

2 good handfuls of dried apricots

Salt and pepper to taste

Heat the oil in a casserole or pan large enough to take all the ingredients and fry the onions gently until they are beginning to soften. Add the cayenne and paprika and the meat. Fry gently until the pieces are lightly browned. Add the apricots and tomatoes. Cover the casserole, bring it to the boil, reduce the heat immediately, cover the dish and either simmer very slowly on the top of the stove or cook gently in the oven *(preheated to 140C/fan 120/gas 1)* for at least 2 hours.

The casserole is ready when the meat is tender. This dish can be cooked very successfully in a slow cooker. Serve with rice boiled with a half a teaspoonful of turmeric, and a green salad.

THE GOOD WINE SHOP RECOMMENDS
Château de Gaure, Cuvée pour Mon Père, Limoux.
A 'natural' red wine made with minimal addition of sulphur, this is a unique wine in which not all the sugar is turned to alcohol, giving a marvellously generous mouthful of rich brambly fruit that will complement the apricot in this dish.

Rose veal burgers with chorizo

The delicate texture of the veal combined with the spicy Spanish chorizo makes a tender, flavourful burger.

Makes 4 medium burgers

400g veal mince

50g chorizo, chopped as fine as you can

1 small red onion, peeled and chopped fine

Salt and pepper to taste

Mix all the ingredients together and add salt and pepper. Divide the mix into four parts. Wet your hands (this will prevent the mix sticking to them) and shape the burgers. Chill them in the fridge for at least 20 minutes.

Grill, fry or barbecue them for around 3 minutes each side.

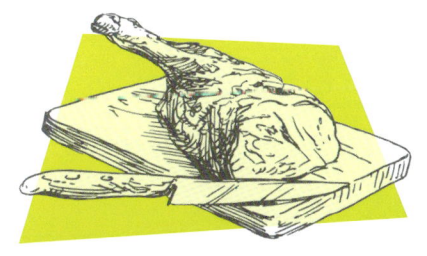

THE GOOD WINE SHOP RECOMMENDS
Côtes du Rhône Rouge 'Point de Folie', Val d'Garrigue, Southern Rhone.
This classic Côtes du Rhône, 'Point de Folie' – 'the edge of madness' – has a nose of red fruit aromas, morello cherries and wild strawberries. The palate is loaded with ripe dark, spicy and berry fruit. With an elegant structure, it is soft, round and mouth-filling.

Rose veal meatballs in a spicy tomato sauce

Serve these delicate yet spicy meatballs with rice, pasta, or potatoes – they would be equally good.

Serves 4

For the meatballs

400g rose veal mince
2 long shallots, peeled and chopped fine
2 tsp capers
2 tbs olive oil

For the tomato sauce

500ml dry white wine
400g chopped tomatoes, fresh or tinned
1–2 tsp sugar
Large pinch cayenne pepper
Large pinch paprika
Salt and pepper
Chopped parsley

Mix all the meatball ingredients together. Wet your hands and make the balls – they should be about the size of a walnut. Heat the oil in a pan large enough to contain all the ingredients, meatballs and sauce. First fry the meatballs – just a quick fry until they are golden, then take them out, as they'll do the rest of their cooking in the sauce.

Then add the white wine and boil it until the volume has reduced by half. Add the tomatoes, sugar, cayenne pepper and paprika, bring back to the boil and add the meatballs. Cover the pan and simmer for 10 minutes or so, until the meatballs are cooked through. Check for pepper and salt and scatter parsley on the top.

Ossobuco

Here's a classic Italian dish from the northern region of Emilia-Romagna. Chris Stileman sells this cut of veal as 'Ossobuco' – the translation into English is 'bone with a hole'.

Serves 6–8

40g plain flour sieved with ½ tsp salt and ground pepper
1kg 'Ossobuco' veal shin
4 tbs olive oil
1 large onion, peeled and finely sliced
3 carrots, peeled and diced fine
3 celery stalks, chopped
4 bay leaves
100ml dry white wine
1 litre stock, beef or vegetable
4 sage leaves
1 sprig of rosemary
Grated rind of 1 orange
Salt and pepper

Put the flour, salt and pepper in a plastic bag large enough to take the veal. Shake the veal in the bag so that all pieces of meat are coated with the flour. Heat the oil in a large pan or casserole. Fry the coated veal until it is golden. Take the meat from the pan and set aside. Fry the onion, carrot, celery and bay leaves until the onion is beginning to soften. Add the wine, stock, sage, rosemary and orange rind and put back the veal. Bring the casserole back to a simmer, check for salt and pepper, cover and either simmer gently on top of the stove or in the oven *(preheated to 140C/fan 120C/gas 1)* for a minimum of 2 hours.

If you are lucky enough to have a slow cooker, this is a perfect recipe for it. The longer and slower the meat cooks, the better – it should fall off the bones. Serve it with steamed or boiled rice and lots of crusty bread to mop up the sauce.

> **THE GOOD WINE SHOP RECOMMENDS**
> **Bruno Giacosa, Dolcetto d'Alba, from Piedmont, Italy.**
> Appealing and fragrant with a bright bouquet of red fruit mingled with aromas of violets. The palate is full of vibrant blackberry and cherry with elegant notes of dried herbs.

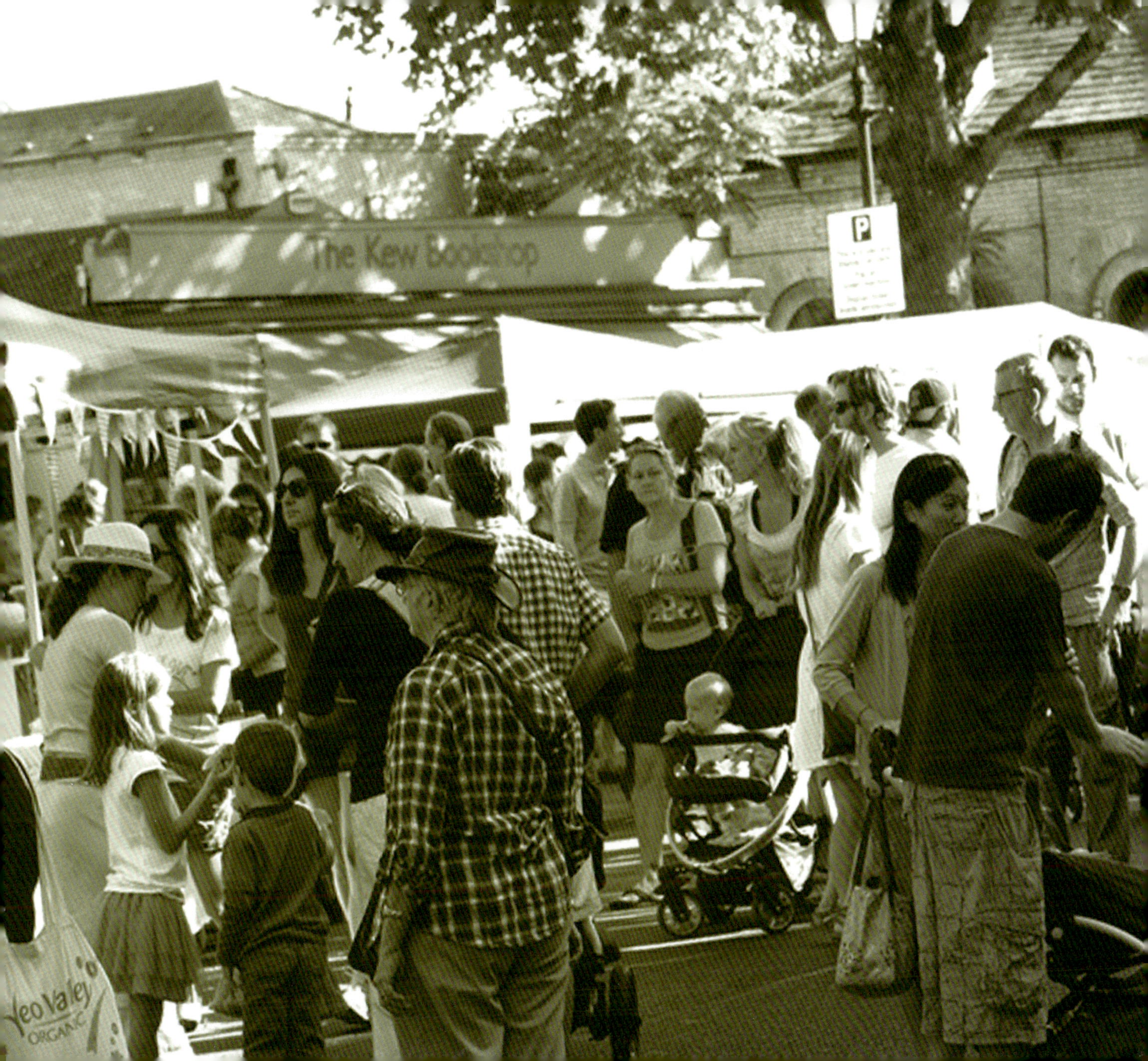
The Kew Bookshop
P
Yeo Valley
ORGANIC

from Strawberry Dream

Brazilian-born chocolatier Isabel Amorim uses a range of exotic ingredients from her home country to hand-make her exquisite, unique chocolates.

When she was starting out she made a chocolate-covered strawberry which a friend described as 'a strawberry dream' – so that's what she called her company.

Brigadeiro

These sweeties taste like truffles, but different. Keep them covered in the fridge and pop them into tiny foil or paper cups to serve. Guaranteed success!

Makes 40

400g condensed milk

A knob of unsalted butter

30g cocoa powder or drinking chocolate

To finish: chocolate strands or cocoa powder

Combine the condensed milk, butter and cocoa in a saucepan (preferably non-stick) over a low heat, stirring continuously with a wooden spoon. Allow the mixture to cook gently for about 2–3 minutes, then take the pan off the heat. Beat the mixture vigorously with a wooden spoon. When it starts to thicken, pour it onto a plate.

When it is cool enough to handle, roll small balls of the mixture, about the size of a cherry, in either cocoa powder or chocolate strands before storing them in the fridge.

SCOTCH EGGS SAUSAGE ROLLS £3.50
PORK PIES £4.00 each

£2.50 per slice

A. V. SCOTLAND FARM

from Sugarmaddy Cakes

Madeline Hillman and her husband Alan were Kew Village Market pioneers: as an original committee member he helped to set up and run it, and she was one of our first stallholders. Sugarmaddy's stall was always laden with the most tempting baked treats, including the prettiest Cake Pops which would draw clusters of children trying to decide which to choose.

The Hillmans have recently moved from Kew and therefore from the market, sadly for us. However, Madeline is still baking – visit her website (www.sugarmaddycakes.co.uk) to see her beautiful 'occasion cakes', made to order for the big days in our lives – big birthdays, weddings and christenings – and all decorated with her exquisite hand-made sugar flowers. Here, however, are some humbler treats, recipes from Madeline that are achievable by the novice baker. All very English, very scrumptious.

Gluten- & wheat-free cupcakes

Madeline says, 'I often make these for children's birthday parties, so that everyone can enjoy a cupcake.'

Makes about 20 cupcakes

150g butter
150g caster sugar
3 eggs, beaten until fluffy
A drop of vanilla essence
150g self-raising gluten- and wheat-free flour (Madeline uses Doves Farm), sifted
3 tbs milk
2 tbs water
125g icing sugar
1 tbs water or lemon or orange juice

Preheat the oven to 160C/ fan 140/gas 3.

Beat together the butter and sugar until light in colour and fluffy in texture. Gradually add the beaten eggs, vanilla essence, and a little of the flour. Fold in the remainder of the flour and the milk and 2tbs water. (Don't worry if it looks very liquid.)

Place paper cases in a patty tin and half-fill them with the cake mixture. Bake for approximately 10–15 minutes. Allow the cupcakes to cool on a wire rack.

Sift the icing sugar into a bowl. Gradually add the water or juice to make it thick enough to cover the back of a spoon. Spread over the top of each cupcake and leave to set. If you are making these with children, they can decorate the cakes with sugar strands.

Tiger cake

A tiger-striped cake is a big hit. On its cake plate it looks very plain, even slightly mundane, but when you cut it – wow! Children love it and even grown-ups ooh and aah.

250ml corn oil
250 caster sugar
100ml milk
4 eggs
300g self-raising flour, sifted
½ tsp vanilla essence
1 tsp baking powder
25g cocoa powder, sieved
1 tbs marmalade, sieved

Preheat the oven to 180C/ fan 160/gas 4.

Line a 24cm round cake tin with baking paper. Beat together the oil, sugar, milk and eggs until the mixture is thick and frothy. This should take about 10 minutes. Divide this mixture equally into two bowls. In one bowl, add 175g sifted flour, ½ tsp vanilla essence and ½ tsp baking powder and mix together. In the other bowl add 125g sifted flour, ½ tsp baking powder, the cocoa powder and the marmalade and mix together.

Place a tablespoon of the vanilla mix in the centre of the cake tin. Using a clean spoon, add a tablespoon of the chocolate mixture on top of the vanilla. Continue to alternate the mixtures until they are both used up.

Important – do not stir or mix the cake mixture in the tin! It is runny enough to spread on its own and when cooked the tiger stripes will appear.

Bake for 45 minutes. Test by inserting a steel skewer in the top. If it comes out sticky, then the cake needs another few minutes.

Remove from the tin and turn out on to a wire rack to cool. Serve on its own or with whipped cream and wait for the compliments!

Marmalade ice-cream

I have left the recipe as Madeline gave it to me because it is a great one for a party, but it works just as well if you make half the amount.

Makes 8-10 portions
8 egg yolks
225g caster sugar
600ml double cream
100g marmalade

Whip the yolks with the sugar until they are pale, light and fluffy. In a separate bowl, large enough to hold all the ingredients, whip the cream until it just holds its shape. Fold the marmalade into the cream very gently – you want to keep the air in the mixture. Then fold the whipped sugar and egg mixture into the cream and marmalade and mix very lightly.

Put it into an ice-cream maker if you have one. If not, put the bowlful of mixture into the freezer for a couple of hours; then take it out and stir it to stop crystals forming; then return it to the freezer until you want to serve it. Ideally, take it out an hour or so before serving – it makes it easier to scoop out.

Sugarmaddy's simple fruit cake

This is the easiest of cakes and one which children really enjoy making. You don't even need scales. Use a large coffee- or tea-cup to measure all of the ingredients.

3 cups self-raising flour, sifted
1 cup of sugar
1 cup of milk
3 eggs, lightly beaten
1 cup of corn oil
2 cups of mixed dried fruit
1 pinch of mixed spice
1 tbs honey for glazing

Preheat the oven to 160C/ fan 140/gas 3.

Grease or oil a 1 litre oblong loaf tin and line it with baking paper. Put all of the ingredients except the honey in a large bowl and beat for 2 minutes with a wooden spoon. Turn the mix into the loaf tin, place the tin on a baking sheet and bake in the centre of the oven for 1¼ hours. The cake is done when a metal skewer comes out of the cake clean. If it still looks sticky, let it have 5–10 minutes longer.

Allow to cool for 10 minutes and then turn it out onto a wire rack, brush the top with honey and leave until cold. This is nice served as it is, or sliced and spread with butter.

THE GOOD WINE SHOP RECOMMENDS
Lustau East India Solero Sherry, Spain
Take a hint from our forebears who drank fortified wines with their sweetmeats. From a distinguished producer, this is an award-winning sherry, reminiscent of rich, concentrated fig and raisin fruits.

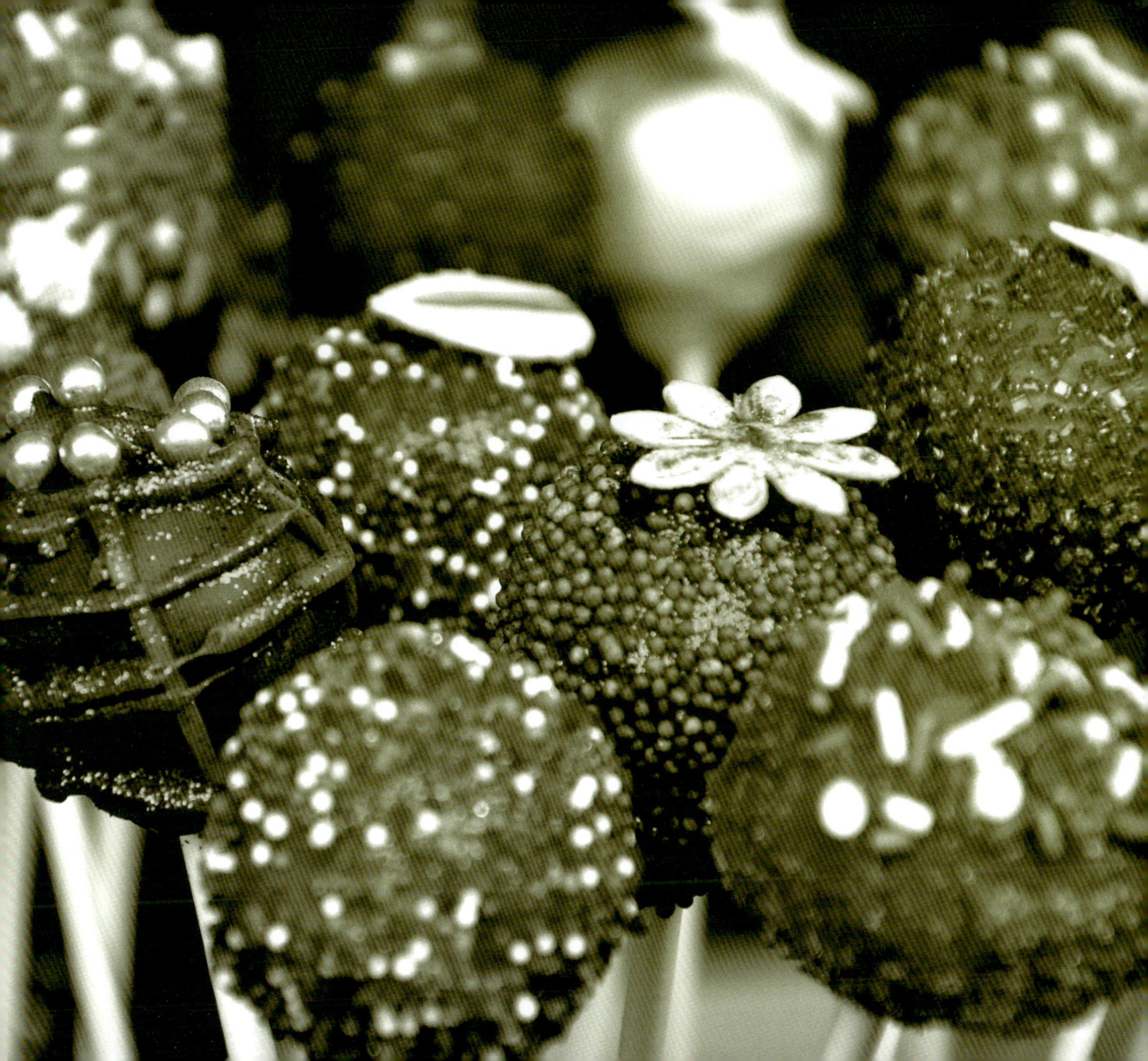

from Thee Olive Tree

This stall is a food lover's heaven: 23 different types of stuffed and marinated olives, marinated feta in olive oil, feta-stuffed red pepelino peppers, sun-blushed and sun-dried tomatoes, artichokes in oil, hummus, tapenade, stuffed vine leaves, anchovies, red and green pesto, harissa and marinated garlic. And at the right time of year, wonderful fresh heads of garlic. (Visit their website www.theeolivetree.co.uk to find out all about their range.) Nearly all the stock is housed in handsome wooden tubs. The whole stall is a delight, a feast for the eyes as well as for the stomach.

Olives are a staple of Mediterranean cuisines and I have raided French, Italian, and Moroccan food traditions for recipes using them.

Pissaladière

France's answer to the Italian pizza!

Serves 6

300g ready-made puff pastry

1kg onions, peeled (this may seem a lot of onions, but they do reduce when they cook)

175ml olive oil

2 cloves of garlic, peeled

8 anchovy fillets

2 tbs milk

8 black olives

Preheat the oven to 180C/ fan 160/gas 4.

Roll out the pastry to form an oblong 34cm x 24cm and put it on a baking tray. Slice the onions and cook them gently in a shallow pan in half the olive oil until very soft. This can take up to 30 minutes. After 15 minutes, mince the garlic and add it to the onions. Give the pan a stir from time to time so that the mixture cooks evenly.

While they are cooking, soak the anchovies in the milk, drain them and pat them dry. Spread the onions on the pastry base, leaving a 3cm border round the edge. Cut the anchovies in half lengthways and use them to make a criss-cross pattern over the onions. Put an olive in each square and dribble the remaining olive oil on the top.

Bake for approximately 40–45 minutes – you want the pastry to be crisp. Cut into squares and serve hot or warm.

Pasta with olives, anchovies & capers

This is a store-cupboard recipe – the ingredients can be kept in stock at home and made into this delicious pasta when you are in a hurry or tired. If you happen to have parsley, spring onions or basil, chop a large handful into the pasta when you toss it.

Serves 2

50g black olives, stoned
4 anchovy fillets
50g sun-dried tomatoes
1 tbs capers, rinsed
3 tbs extra virgin olive oil
300g short pasta, such as fusilli, farfalle or penne
Freshly grated Parmesan cheese

THE GOOD WINE SHOP RECOMMENDS
Ciu Ciu 'Bacchus' Rosso Picen, Marche, Italy. This is a juicy red wine, bursting with flavours of red cherries, bright raspberries and liquorice. A simple and uncomplicated wine to go with simple Italian dishes. It would also suit the chicken dish on the next page.

Roughly chop the olives, anchovies and the tomatoes and add the capers. Warm the olive oil in a shallow pan and stir in all the ingredients except the pasta and Parmesan. Let the ingredients warm through gently – be careful not to let the mix become too hot.

Cook the pasta in boiling salted water until it is *al dente* (usually about 10 minutes – see the packet instructions).

Drain and tip into a warmed serving bowl. Pour over the sauce, stir gently and serve. Grated Parmesan is the perfect finish to this deliciously piquant pasta.

Tapenade

A tangy French olive and anchovy spread – serve it on thin slices of toasted French bread either with aperitifs or as a first course.

175g black olives, stoned
175g capers
75g anchovy fillets, soaked for 10 minutes in 2tbs milk
75g tinned tuna, drained
1 tbs mustard powder
200ml olive oil
½ tps each of black pepper, ground cloves, nutmeg

Put the stoned olives in a food processor with the capers, the soaked and drained anchovy fillets, the tuna and the mustard powder. Process till it's a smooth paste then gradually add the oil, drop by drop, as if making mayonnaise.

Turn it into a bowl and stir in the spices. Pile the tapenade into a jar and cover. It will keep for two weeks in the fridge.

Moroccan chicken with green olives & lemon

Some of Moroccan cuisine's essential ingredients feature here — lemon, spices and of course the olives. The effect is fragrant but not hot-spicy.

Serves 4

- 2 lemons
- 2 tbs olive oil
- 1 large onion, peeled and sliced thin
- Approx. 4cm ginger, peeled and chopped fine
- 2 cloves of garlic, peeled
- 2 tsp paprika
- 2 tsp cumin seeds
- 1 tsp cinnamon
- 500ml chicken or vegetable stock
- 8 chicken thighs, skin removed
- Salt and pepper
- 150g green olives, pitted
- Chopped fresh coriander to serve

Cut one lemon into 8 wedges. Squeeze the juice from second lemon. Set the wedges and juice aside.

Heat the olive oil in a pan large enough to take all the ingredients and fry the onion and ginger gently until soft and golden. This will probably take about 10 minutes. Crush the garlic into the onions and add the paprika, cumin and cinnamon. Stir well and fry for another 3–5 minutes. Add the stock and bring the mixture to the boil. Sprinkle the chicken pieces with salt and pepper and add to the pan. Reduce the heat, cover the pan, and simmer until the chicken is cooked through. (This should take approximately 20–25 minutes.) Keep an eye on it and turn the chicken pieces occasionally.

Transfer the chicken to a shallow dish and keep it warm. Add the olives and lemon juice to the sauce and boil uncovered for five minutes to thicken slightly. Season with salt and pepper and pour the sauce over the chicken. Scatter chopped coriander over the dish and serve with rice or couscous and a couple of lemon wedges each to squeeze over the dish.

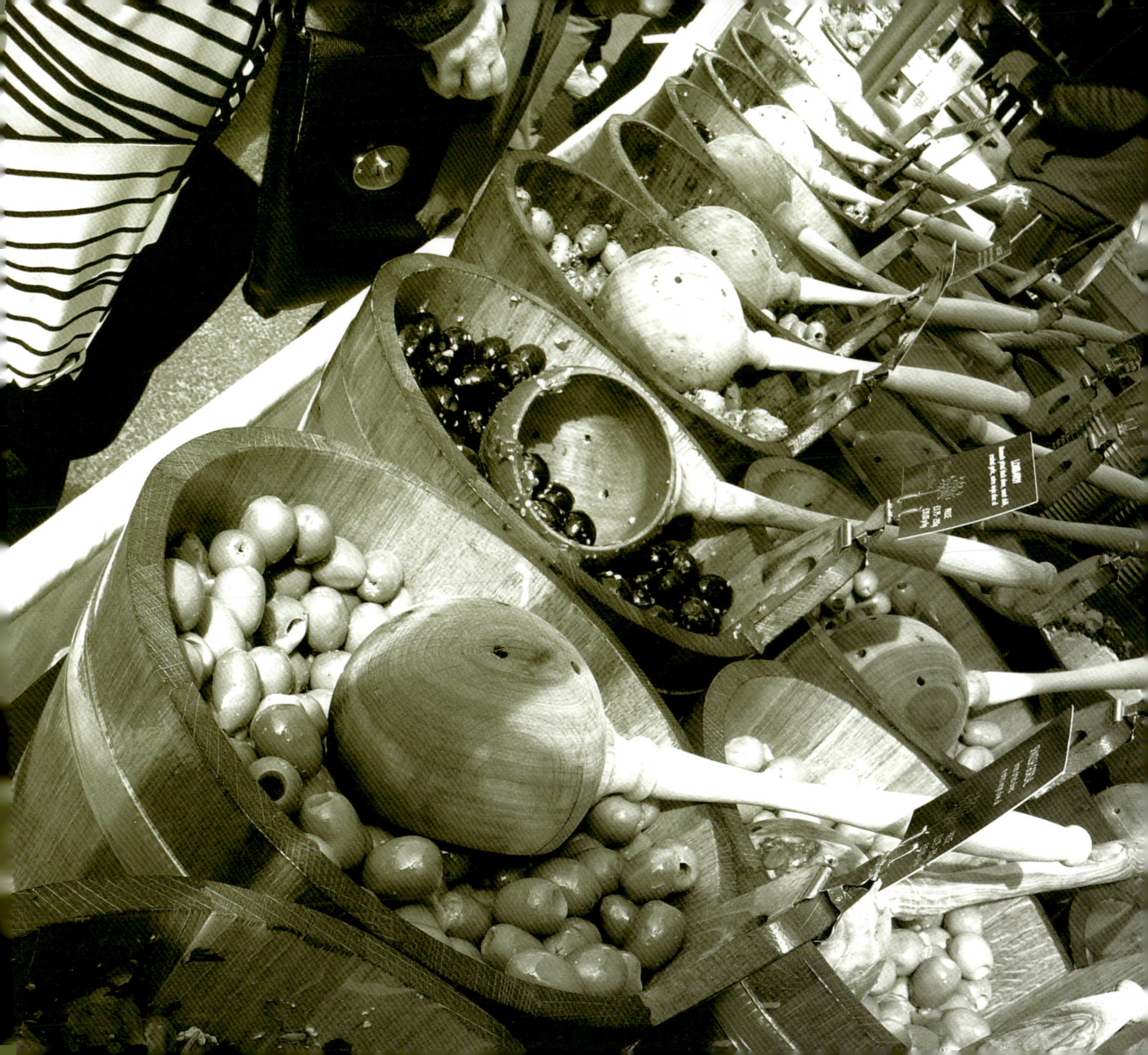

from
Winterbourne Game

Chris Norcott specialises in the best seasonal game. Rabbit, pigeon, venison and pheasant all appear on his stall and he also has a line in tasty venison sausages and pies.

Venison and pigeon are in season all the year round, so the recipes given here are achievable during any month. Venison cooked slowly in red wine is rich and rewarding. Venison Chilli is unusual and exotic – it works brilliantly, the 'hit' of the chilli contrasting with the rich meat. And a haunch of Chris's venison is real celebration food.

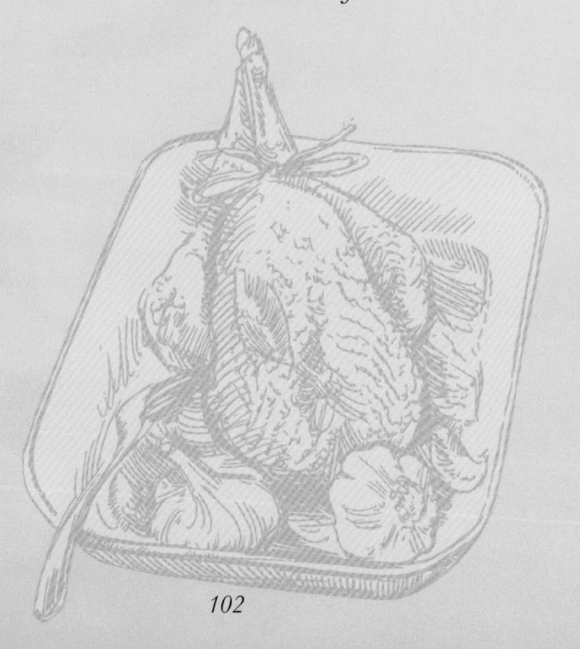

Roast haunch of venison

This is not a recipe but rather information on what size of haunch you need for the number of people you are feeding, oven temperature and time of cooking. I find detailed instructions like these invaluable when faced with a piece of meat I have never cooked before and which I don't want to spoil by under- or over-cooking. A haunch is cooked 'bone in' so allow at least 300g per person.

1 haunch of venison
2 tbs olive oil
Pepper and salt

Preheat the oven to 200C/fan 180/gas 6.

REAL ALE LTD RECOMMENDS
Kernel Export Stout 1890, 7.2%. Winner of the International Beer Challenge 2011, this is a dark and rich stout brewed to an 1890 recipe.

Brush or wipe over the joint with olive oil and pepper and salt it. Add the rest of the olive oil to the roasting tin and preheat it. Place the haunch in the tin and brown the joint all over. Then roast the haunch for 10–15 minutes on high heat to 'seal' the meat.

Take out the joint and turn the oven down to *180C/fan 160C/gas 4*. When the heat has subsided, return the joint to the oven and roast for a further 15 minutes per 400 grams.

Remove it from the oven, cover the joint with foil and rest the meat for 10–15 minutes before carving.

Chunky venison chilli

You can make this chilli ahead of time and keep it in the fridge until the next day – it tastes even better rested and reheated.

Serves 4-6

1 tbs vegetable oil

4 medium onions, peeled and sliced

2 chillis, seeds removed and chopped finely, or ½ tsp chilli flakes

500g diced venison

400g tin of chopped tomatoes

1 tsp Worcester sauce

100ml red wine

1 beef stock cube dissolved in 100 ml water

Salt and pepper

400 tin red kidney beans, drained and rinsed

Preheat the oven to 140C/ fan 120/gas 1.

Heat the oil in a pan or stewpot which will go in the oven and fry the onions gently for about 5 minutes. Add the chopped chillis or chilli flakes, and the diced venison and fry until all are nicely browned. Then add the chopped tomatoes, the Worcester sauce, red wine and stock and season with salt and pepper.

Bring the chilli to the boil, take it off the heat, cover it and place it in the oven for 1½ hours, gently braising it until the venison is tender. Then add the kidney beans to the casserole, bring it back up to the boil and simmer it for 30 minutes so the beans absorb the flavour.

Serve either on its own or with plain boiled rice. Some bread to mop up the gravy and a green salad also go very well.

REAL ALE LTD RECOMMENDS
Downton Chimera Dark Delight, 6%.
Dark, complex and strong but subtle with a hint of chocolate and coffee beans.

Pigeon breasts and toasted goat's cheese

Chris likes to eat these with sweet chilli sauce – the sweet sharp taste of the sauce contrasts well with the rich creamy cheese. And why not buy your goat's cheese for the stuffing from the Nut Knowle Farm stall at the market?

Serves 4 as a light lunch

4 thick slices of granary bread

4 tbs olive oil

8 pigeon breasts

8 slices of goat's cheese

100g rocket leaves

Preheat the grill.

Brush the bread with olive oil both sides and toast under the grill. Set aside while you cook the pigeon breasts. Heat the rest of the oil in a frying pan and fry the pigeon breasts for about 2 minutes each side.

Put two pigeon breasts on each toast, top with a slice of goat's cheese and return to the grill until the cheese starts to melt. Lay each toast on a plate, scatter rocket over the dish and serve immediately.

REAL ALE LTD RECOMMENDS:
Little Beer Corporation Little Snug, 5.4%.
Warm, full-bodied, mellow with fruit and biscuit flavours in the centre and a little smokiness on the edge. It has a honey colour and the fresh aroma of hay and earthy hops.

Slow braise of venison & vegetables with red wine

I cooked this on a cold autumn day and the meat had a rich yet subtle flavour. Absolutely delicious!

Serves 4

- 400–500g diced venison (depends how hungry you are!)
- 2 tbs plain flour, mixed with a pinch of salt, 1 tsp fresh thyme (or ½ tsp dried) and black pepper to taste
- 2 tbs olive or sunflower oil
- 4 medium onions, peeled and quartered
- 4 medium carrots, peeled and cut in thick chunks
- 4 medium potatoes, peeled and cut into thick chunks
- 2 bay leaves
- 300ml red wine
- 300ml beef stock (a cube is fine)
- 1 tbs Worcester sauce
- Salt and pepper

Preheat the oven to 140C/fan 120/gas 1.

Coat the venison in the seasoned flour. (An easy way to do this is to put the flour in a plastic bag with the diced venison and shake the bag until all the meat is coated.) Heat the oil and fry the meat until nicely browned.

Remove the meat and set it aside while you fry the onions, carrots and potatoes – you may need to add an extra tablespoon of oil. When they too are browned, put half of the vegetables and the meat in an oven-proof casserole with the bay leaves and pour over the red wine, stock and Worcester sauce.

Bring the casserole to the boil on the top of the stove, then cover the pot and place it in the oven. After 2 hours, add the balance of the vegetables and continue braising. This ensures that the meat will be tender and some of the vegetables will still have a bit of a crunch.

After a total 3 hours, take the pot out of the oven, check for seasoning and serve with creamy mustard mash.

> **REAL ALE LTD RECOMMENDS**
> **Kernel Export Stout 1890, 7.2%.**
> Winner of the International Beer Challenge 2011, this is a dark and rich stout brewed to an 1890 recipe.

About Kew Village Market

On the first Sunday of each month – as friends, neighbours and visitors alike flock to browse and buy, meet and eat – Kew Village Market is as much a social hub as a shopping opportunity.

Since its launch on Sunday 2nd October 2011 it's become a well-loved local institution that is:

★ Run by the community – the Committee which organises the market and the volunteers who help to run it are all Kew residents giving their time for free.

★ For the community – with a carefully selected variety of quality fresh foods and unique crafts, it not only offers an alternative to supermarkets and chains but also encourages and supports local small businesses.

★ In aid of community causes – all the operating profits are given to local charities who can also take a stall for free to promote their cause.

If you'd like to find out more, please visit the website www.kewvillagemarket.org where you can sign up for our newsletter and see which stalls will be attending each month.

KEW VILLAGE MARKET

on the first Sunday of every month (except January) 10am to 2pm

By Kew Gardens tube
Station Parade & Royal Parade
TW9 3PZ

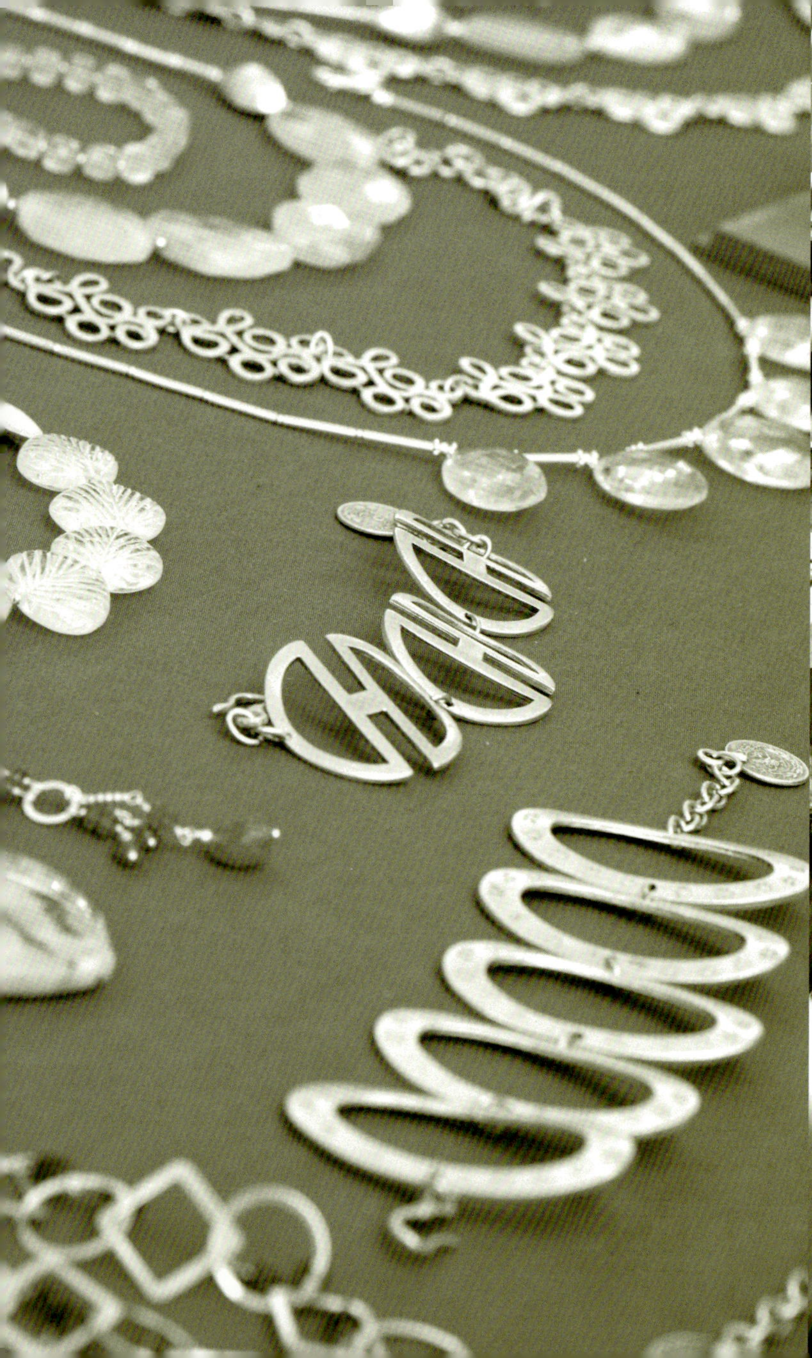

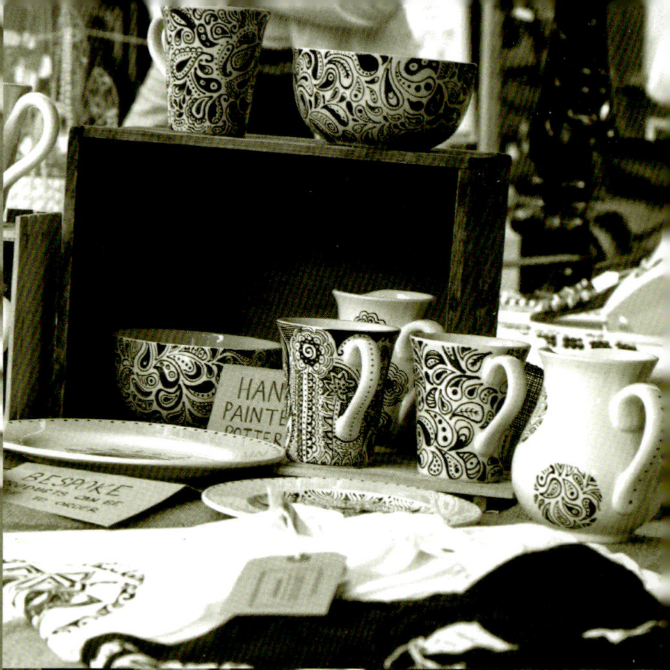
BESPOKE

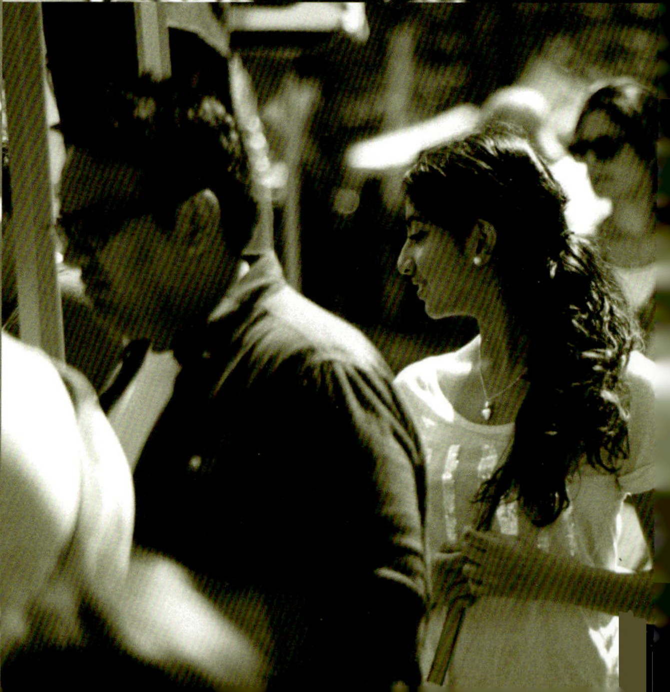

ORANGE ZINGER
Mixed pitted with black & kalamata olives
fresh tomato, orange juice & zest,
crushed garlic, thyme, a sprinkle of seeds
and extra virgin olive oil

PRICE 250g
£3.75
£15.00 p/kg

Index of recipes

SOUPS, STARTERS & LIGHT LUNCHES OR SUPPERS

Beetroot soup with Beenleigh Blue cheese croûtons	67
Caramelised shallots with Fourme d'Ambert on flaky pastry	68
Cheddar cheese & Calvados fondue	67
Chicken liver pâté	48
Goat's cheese & rocket pasta	72
Goat's cheese & vegetable tarts	71
Ham, cheese & leek tart	30
La ribollita	85
Lamb, vegetable & pot barlcy soup	31
Pappa pomodoro	84
Pasta with olives, anchovies & capers	99
Pasta with goat's cheese, courgettes & lemon	72
Pigeon breasts & toasted goat's cheese	103
Pissaladière	98
Potato, Reblochon cheese & pancetta slice	29
Pumpkin, feta, olive & oregano tart	30
Red onion, blue cheese & fig with rocket & walnuts slice	29
Risotto with four cheeses	66
Sardinian pane frattau	86
Savoury crêpes with goat's cheese, walnut & honey filling	38
Smoked salmon pain perdu & salad	40
Spicy hot dry vegetable curry	17
Split green pea & mint soup	76
Sweet potato, chilli, ginger & coconut soup	31
Terrine de campagne	49
Zuppa gallurese	87

MEAT DISHES

Boeuf bourguignon	40
Casseroled lamb with apricots	89
Chicken breasts stuffed with goat's cheese	71
Chunky venison chilli	103
Irish stew	77
Lamb burgers with minty yogurt dressing	88
Medium spicy chicken curry	17
Moroccan chicken with green olives & lemon	100
Ossobuco	90
Pork in cider with a suet pie crust	64
Pork tenderloin carbonara	61
Roast haunch of venison	102
Roast pork belly with a chestnut & anchovy stuffing	62
Rose veal burgers with chorizo	89
Rose veal meatballs in a spicy tomato sauce	90
Sausage & chorizo cassoulet	62
Slow braise of venison & vegetables with red wine	104
Stuffed shoulder of pork with walnut, capers & lemon stuffing	63
Stuffed tenderloin of Lop pork	61
Sweet & sour sticky spare ribs	60

continued

continued

FISH DISHES

Baking fish	13
Baked mullet with white wine	80
Dived scallops in the shell with garlic butter	82
Fish korma with tomatoes	16
Plaki	82
Seafood pie	81

SALADS, SIDE DISHES & VEGETABLEs

Aubergine salad (Baba Ganoush)	14
Beetroot, walnut & goat's cheese salad	70
Broad bean dip	14
Endive salad with Roquefort, celery & walnuts	67
Expert advice on potatoes, squashes & apples	18
Garden vegetable salad with salsa verde	32
Hummus	13
Nutty Lady coleslaw	74
Nutty Lady quinoa, feta & squash salad	75
Pot barley & puy lentil salad	78
Spicy lentil, cauliflower & butternut squash salad with coriander	28
Tapenade	99

PRESERVES & MARINADES

Beat-root chutney	35
Olive oil & vinegar dressing	13
Olive oil marinades	12
Red cabbage pickle	77
Expert tips for perfect preserves	34
Spicy roo chutney	36

PUDDINGS, ICES, SWEETS & DRINKS

Amber & Sophie's rocky roads	22
Brigadeiro	92
Coconut ice	22
Cookie-crumb ice-cream pops	42
Crêpes suzettes	39
Crunchy nut crumble	78
Flax super smoothie	45
Fruit & linseed salad with linseed cream	45
Marmalade ice-cream	95
Sweet crêpes with fruity filling	39
Tiramisu	43

BAKES, CAKES & BISCUITS

Anzacs	58
Brazilian cheese puff breads	55
Cannoli siciliana	25
Cantucci di prato	24
Chocolate éclairs or profiteroles	51
Chorizo breads	54
Flax Farm flapjacks	44
Gluten- & dairy-free florentines	58
Gluten- & wheat-free cupcakes	94
Lemon tarts	50
Lusobrazil pineapple upside-down cake	55
Macaroons with chocolate ganache or coffee buttercream	56
Millionaire cookie bars	43
Sugarmaddy's simple fruit cake	96
Tiger cake	95